What others are saying about *Simply Strategic Stuff*...

"Tim and Tony have developed a practical 'how-to' primer that will prove to be a handy reference not only for church administrators, but for anyone involved in church leadership. The School of Hard Knocks has just generated a diploma, and it's called *Simply Strategic Stuff*. Get a copy for every key member of your staff."

— **Dr. David Foster,** Senior Pastor, Bellevue Community Church

"Granger Community Church is one of the best-run churches in the country. I wish I would have had this simple but practical guide when I taught church leadership at Reformed Theological Seminary, Orlando. For that matter, I wish I would have had it during the stages of my own church's growth! Stevens and Morgan give guidance for leadership in any size church, in any denomination or situation. I really like the thought-sized format. What is most helpful, though, is the practical and applicational truth of church management."

— **Dr. Joel C. Hunter,** Senior Pastor, Northland—A Church Distributed

"The title has it right. *Simply Strategic Stuff* is a quick read of 99 practical handles for church administration that get to the heart of the matter quickly. Tim Stevens and Tony Morgan, pastors on staff at Granger Community Church, write of what they have experienced. They deal with everything from 'using more bytes and less paper' to 'when you discover sin in the leadership, don't cover it up.' What they have written is a practical handbook (especially for pastors in their first or second churches) that should be handy on the desk and will soon be well worn. This book is delightful, practical, and rich with doable suggestions, and it focuses on hard issues in church administration made easy. In the words of the authors, 'This book compiles a number of simple strategies...to allow us to reach more people for Jesus.' I recommend it highly."

— **Bishop James R. King Jr.,** Louisville Area (Kentucky and Red Bird Conferences), The United Methodist Church

"*Simply Strategic Stuff* will be a tremendous help to pastors and church leaders. Tim Stevens and Tony Morgan have put together creative answers to difficult questions and innovative ways of enlarging the ministry of the local church. Their suggestions are very practical and doable. Their ideas will ignite your creative energies to deal with these opportunities and others as they arise in your local situation. I highly commend it."

— **John Ed Mathison,** Senior Minister, Frazer, A United Methodist Congregation

"Tony and Tim give practical answers to questions every church leader is asking. This is the best 'how to' leadership book I have read and will be required reading for all our management team leaders."

— **Bob Merritt,** Senior Pastor, Eagle Brook Church

"Tim Stevens and Tony Morgan take the mystery out of church administration and show how exciting strategies in the local church can make a difference for the Kingdom. *Simply Strategic Stuff* is not just good content; it is fun reading as well!"

—**Dr. Thom S. Rainer,** Dean, Southern Baptist Theological Seminary; President, The Rainer Group Church Consultants

"*Simply Strategic Stuff* lives up to its title! Never before have I seen one resource that tackles so many key areas of administration for growing churches. Tony and Tim provide valuable answers and strategies gained from their firsthand experience. Particularly helpful is the area of employee and staffing procedures...things like how to keep employees fulfilled, what to do when good employees go bad, how to handle moral failure on your staff, and how and when to hire new employees. This book answers the questions churches are asking!"

—**Todd A. Rhoades,** ChurchStaffing.com

"Tim and Tony have done a fine job of making the nuts and bolts of day-to-day church administration not just clear but practical. If you are looking for a handbook of battle-tested principles on how to strengthen what's under the hood of your local church, this is your book."

—**J. David Schmidt,** President, J. David Schmidt & Associates

"*Simply Strategic Stuff* is an insider's viewpoint into the workings of a highly effective church. Far from dry, this is vital stuff that I wish I had my hands on years ago. It would have saved me a lot of heartache. It isn't very often that one gets the opportunity to get a sneak peek into the heart and mind of a church like Granger, but here you have it in one handy volume."

—**Steve Sjogren,** Founding Pastor, Vineyard Community Church, Cincinnati, Ohio

"Few books are named as well as *Simply Strategic Stuff*—because that is exactly what this is! Tim and Tony have just saved thousands of pastors, staff members, and church leaders tons of pain and heartache. We have needed a book that deals with the nuts and bolts of doing church for a long time—and now we have it!"

—**Dan Southerland,** Director, Church Transitions

"It's easy to become so consumed with doing church that we don't slow down long enough to evaluate what we're doing. Tim and Tony have done some thinking for us all. *Simply Strategic Stuff* is full of innovative ideas to help you programmatically and strategically."

—**Andy Stanley,** Senior Pastor, North Point Community Church

Additional Resources

This book was written to help pastors and other leaders implement ministry infrastructure that encourages spiritual and church growth. Many other resources intended for this purpose are available through WiredChurches, a ministry of Granger Community Church in Granger, Indiana.

Over the past several years, church staff and volunteer leaders have frequented www.wiredchurches.com and training events hosted on the Granger campus to learn more about the church's ministry strategy. Here are a number of ways WiredChurches is prepared to train and equip you and your team.

Innovative Church Conference

The Innovative Church Conference is offered each year to provide cutting-edge communications, media, and leadership principles for the church. Learn from the recent experiences of the Granger team, and hear from the leading voices in America today. This conference will provide your team with the latest thoughts and trends on our culture and the church. Together, we will learn, we will dream, and we will be inspired.

Simply Strategic Workshop

Tim and Tony host a one-day workshop several times throughout the year to dig more deeply into the concepts offered in this book. Spend time with them on the Granger campus (or ask about hosting it at your location), and see firsthand how these principles have been implemented. This highly interactive workshop will give you a chance to ask questions about how these principles apply to your ministry setting.

WiredChurches Workshops

In addition to the Simply Strategic workshop, Granger's staff leaders present several other seminars throughout the year on specific ministry topics such as creative arts, facilities management, small groups, and first impressions.

WiredChurches Resources

WiredChurches provides many useful resources for church leaders, including message subscriptions, leadership downloads, small-group materials, and music. For ordering information, call 1-888-249-6480 or visit www.wiredchurches.com.

Consulting and Speaking

WiredChurches is your connection to personalized consulting, training, and speaking opportunities offered by the key leaders of Granger Community Church. Contact WiredChurches to tap into expert advice on topics such as strategic planning, organizational development, construction planning, first impressions, missions outreach, children's ministry, student ministry, and creative arts.

WiredChurches Web Site (www.wiredchurches.com)

WiredChurches.com has the most current information available about conferences, workshops, new leadership resources, and insights about the ministry of Granger Community Church. Log on today to learn more and to subscribe to our free e-newsletter.

WiredChurches
630 East University Drive
Granger, IN 46530
Phone: 1-888-249-6480
Fax: 574-243-3510
Web: www.wiredchurches.com

wiredChurches.com

foreword by
John C. Maxwell

Simply
Strategic
stuff

Help for Leaders
Drowning in the Details
of Running a Church

TIM **STEVENS**
TONY **MORGAN**

Flagship church resources
from Group Publishing

Simply Strategic Stuff

Help for Leaders Drowning in the Details of Running a Church
Copyright © 2004 Tim Stevens and Tony Morgan

Visit our Web site: **www.grouppublishing.com**

Credits
Creative Development Editor: Paul Woods
Chief Creative Officer: Joani Schultz
Editor: Candace McMahan
Copy Editor: Loma Huh
Art Director: Kari K. Monson
Print Production Artist: Joyce Douglas
Illustrator: Dave Klug
Cover Art Director/Designer: Jeff A. Storm
Production Manager: Peggy Naylor

Unless otherwise noted, Scripture taken from the HOLY BIBLE, NEW INTERNATIONAL VERSION®. Copyright © 1973, 1978, 1984 by International Bible Society. Used by permission of Zondervan Publishing House. All rights reserved.

Library of Congress Cataloging-in-Publication Data
Stevens, Tim, 1967-
    Simply strategic stuff : help for leaders drowning in the details of running a church / by Tim Stevens and Tony Morgan.
        p.   cm.
    Includes bibliographical references and index.
    ISBN 0-7644-2625-7 (alk. paper)
    1. Church management. I. Morgan, Tony, 1968- II. Title.
        BV652.S69 2003
        254--dc21

                                                                    2003013454

10 9 8 7 6 5 4 3   13 12 11 10 09 08 07 06 05 04

Printed in the United States of America.

Contents

Dedication

We are dedicating this book to our pastor, our boss, and our friend—Mark Beeson. Seventeen years ago, in a denomination that favors stability and tradition, he struck out on his own in a very non-traditional way to start a local church. Since then he has built an organization that favors thinking outside of the box. Rather than being intimidated by the strengths of others, he has welcomed and even encouraged those who have complementary gifts. He has led the congregation to be lifelong learners and has championed the value of helping resource other church leaders.

We have learned so many of the concepts contained in this book from Mark. Directly, he has taught us leadership principles. Indirectly, he has provided numerous learning opportunities and allowed us to experiment and explore as we have, together, built the church. He has made a place for our unique contributions and has given us freedom to operate in our areas of passion. From watching Mark's life, we have learned more about encouragement, humility, authenticity, leadership, serving, parenting, tenacity, marriage, and attitude.

We will forever be grateful for his impact on our lives.

—Tim Stevens and Tony Morgan
Granger, Indiana

Acknowledgments

To my wife, Emily. Though Jesus completes me, I wouldn't be who I am without you in my life. You're my greatest cheerleader, my best friend, and you'll always be "my girl."

To Matt Harris, Bob Knabel, Tim Magnuson, and Charlie Rhyan. You have marked who I am as a leader and a Christ follower. Matt and Tim, I'm especially grateful for how you've fueled my passion for the local church.

To Mom and Dad. Thank you for modeling compassionate leadership, encouraging me to create, and instilling the value of doing all things well.

—Tony Morgan

To Faith, my wife of thirteen years. You are the greatest mother and wife on the planet! I'm still madly in love with you, and I'm grateful for your encouragement and support throughout our lives together.

To Lynda Wessel, Lewie Clark, Danny Jones, Greg Bishop, and my parents, Ross and Karen Stevens. Thank you for seeing leadership potential within me when I was young and stupid and for pouring hours of mentoring into my life.

—Tim Stevens

To Doug Slaybaugh, Andrew Accardy, Rick Warren, and our other ministry partners at Saddleback. Thank you for presenting the opportunity for us to launch this project.

To Paul Woods, Candace McMahan, and the entire editorial team at Group Publishing. We appreciate your contributions to this book. More important, we praise God for your ministry to church leaders throughout the country.

To Scott Anderson, Mickey Aquilino, Brian Davis, Kristin Davis, Patrick McGoldrick, Emily Morgan, David Poole, and Greg Whiting. Thank you for your honest input and additional insights.

To Rob Wegner, Mark Waltz, Karen Schuelke, Mark Beeson, and the entire staff at Granger. There's no place on earth we'd rather be!

To the entire congregation at Granger Community Church. You are a joy to lead and serve beside. Your impact is being felt in our city and around the world!

Finally, Lord Jesus, we acknowledge your position in our lives and in our ministry, and we give this book to you with the prayer that you'll use it to bless your church and change lives for eternity.

—Tony Morgan and Tim Stevens

Foreword

"How can I help my ministry grow?" "How can I help my ministry succeed?" It doesn't matter where I'm speaking, I always hear these two questions. And as a former pastor, I understand the challenges of ministry and the passion that drives those in ministry. Wouldn't it be great if there were an easy, foolproof answer? Of course leadership will play a major role in your success, but what about the day-to-day trials? That's where this book comes in. It will provide you with commonsense insight into the day-to-day decisions leaders in ministry have to make.

Simply Strategic Stuff can save you from some big mistakes and guide you toward ministry success. By providing administrative theory that is practical, and practical application that is doable, *Simply Strategic Stuff* is a powerful tool in making your ministry work.

When I speak to people about leadership, I often talk about catalysts. A catalyst is what I call a get-it-done-and-then-some person. And this book is written by two dynamic catalysts. I've watched Tim Stevens and Tony Morgan prove themselves in ministry at Granger Community Church, under the leadership of my friend Mark Beeson. These guys know leadership.

Granger Community Church has experienced tremendous growth in the past fifteen years. Mark Beeson is Granger's founding pastor, and he has filled his staff with leaders. In 1994 Tim Stevens joined the staff. At that time the church had four hundred people attending. Through innovative leadership and smart strategies, the church quadrupled in four years, at which time Tony Morgan joined the leadership team. Since 1998, attendance has nearly tripled again to over four thousand people attending each weekend. The ability to produce and sustain this growth is due, in large part, to the strategies that are presented in this book.

In *Simply Strategic Stuff*, Tim and Tony offer an approach that can take your church to the next level. This book will help you think strategically so you can effectively lead and manage your teams. It will also help you streamline your processes by suggesting ways to reduce bureaucratic inefficiencies as you lead the day-to-day operations of your ministry. Using the ninety-nine keys for ministry success offered in this book, you and your team can win new battles and gain new ground.

The strategies Tim and Tony deliver in *Simply Strategic Stuff* have proven effective in scores of churches across America. And they will help you succeed in ministry too!

—John C. Maxwell
Founder, The INJOY Group
Atlanta, Georgia

Introduction

In May 2002 we were on the campus of Saddleback Church in Lake Forest, California. We had just finished teaching the "Simply Strategic Stuff: 99 Things You Need to Know" workshop twice. The room had been packed both times, and many had to sit on the floor or stand at the back of the room. Afterward we talked to many of the pastors and church leaders who attended the workshop, and we heard again and again how helpful the material was:

"I wish my whole staff had been sitting here with me."

"Where do I find an administrative pastor who knows this stuff?"

"I've been in ministry for thirty years, and I've never heard this before."

"I pastor a church of two thousand, and if we don't get a grip on some of these strategies, we are going to implode."

Following the workshop, we browsed bookstores for materials and found little to help a church leader with administrative tasks. Then we began to scour the Internet and search other resources. All we found was a huge, gaping hole. We discovered that very few resources are available to help church leaders strategically lead their churches. Yet every church leader is expected to provide administrative leadership. Every youth pastor, every children's pastor, every elder, every secretary, every music pastor, and especially every senior pastor, is looked to as the person who can keep the church (or at least a particular ministry area) organized and out of trouble.

Ask any pastor who went to seminary how many classes on church administration were required or even offered. The typical response is laughter. Yet pastors are required to hire, fire, manage and supervise, oversee large budgets and the construction of buildings and parking lots—all with little or no training and few resources specific to ministry.

Each month we get dozens of phone calls or e-mails asking for advice on administrative and leadership issues. As more people find out about the fruit Granger is experiencing, we are asked more questions about the strategy the church has used to grow from a family of five to over four thousand people who gather each weekend. Church leaders are interested in what we're doing now and even more interested in the steps we've taken along the way to position our church for growth. This book compiles a number of simple strategies we've implemented to allow us to reach more people for Jesus.

Steps That Will Help You

As you're reading the book, keep in mind the following words of advice. First, all of these strategies were implemented over the first sixteen years of our church's ministry. Some of them may be implemented in your setting immediately. Others will require time. Trying to instantly adopt everything you read would be a recipe for disaster. At Granger, we always talk about helping people take their *next step* toward Christ. Your ministry has a next step as well, but if you want your next step to have lasting impact, you'll need to take it with the consensus of your team. Granted, some of these changes are directed at the individual leader, but some are going to require you to lay the groundwork with your church before you can move forward.

Second, don't expect all of these strategies to work in every church. You need to put each one of them through the filter of your ministry environment and ask, "Will this work here?" We hope you will capture several new ideas that may position your church for reaching more people for Jesus and helping others take faith steps. However, there will be other strategies that just won't fly in your setting. In that case, realize that they would never work, and move on. Pray for wisdom and discernment as you read this book, asking God to point you toward your next step as a leader.

Additionally, you need to know that nothing in this book contains a magic formula for church growth. The psalms make it clear: "Unless the Lord builds the house, its builders labor in vain" (Psalm 127:1). We must continue to trust God and lean not on our own understanding, but by the same token, "Every prudent man acts out of knowledge" (Proverbs 13:16). The Bible provides great insights into principles for leadership, organizational structure, systems, planning, and other strategies that will help us tell more people about Jesus and focus our ministry efforts. Just as we are intentional about plans for our services, outreach, and discipleship, we also need to have plans in place to support these ministry efforts with staff, systems, facilities, technology, and other key infrastructure components. Though addressing these areas does not guarantee growth, it's been our experience that failure to implement appropriate strategies will almost certainly slow or stop growth.

Finally, we're covering ninety-nine different topics in one short, easy-to-read book. As much as we'd like to think this book offers all the answers, it may really only pose all the questions. It contains some details, but not a lot. For example, we'll share our philosophies about campus development. They will give you an overview of how we've approached construction projects, but there's not enough information in these pages for you to build your own facility. You will still need to dig deeper through conversations with your architect, site visits to other churches, and other resources specifically directed at churches who are ready to build. Similarly, you will find general overviews related to areas such as auditing, budget preparation, and Web strategy. We tried to convince our publisher you'd read our thousand-page treatise on ministry strategies, but they put an editor in charge of making sure we keep this volume short and sweet. If you're looking for additional resources, you may want to begin with the information in the back of the book about WiredChurches—a ministry that offers workshops and conference training to equip pastors and church leaders.

Different Types of Learners

Everyone is wired differently. Some people learn by reading, others by listening. Some learn better in a group; others learn better alone. Some are easily distracted; others can tune everything out. Depending on how you're wired, you might want to approach this book in one of several ways:

Front-to-back. You might prefer to read it as if it were a novel... start at the beginning, and read through to the end. Write in it, use a highlighter, and mark the pages you want to revisit.

Reference guide. Or you may wish to use the topical guide at the back of the book to read chapters pertaining to a specific issue you're facing. Each chapter has been written to stand alone and is not dependent on previous chapters.

Group study. Let your whole team benefit together! There are several ways you might do this. You could all read two or three chapters before you meet and then discuss them together. Another idea is for everyone to read the book independently and choose ten favorite chapters. Then compare notes, and set up a time to discuss the hot issues. Just for fun, also talk about the chapters you thought were the most ridiculous—the ones that would never work in your setting. We've provided a discussion guide at the back of the book that will assist your group discussions.

The Stuff Every Church Leader Needs to Know

Our intention is to provide a resource that helps pastors, administrative staff, and volunteer leaders succeed in building prevailing churches. This is the stuff every church leader needs to know. Some of it you've probably considered before. Some of it you'll discount as our attempt to round out the ninety-nine chapters. In any event, we hope you'll find at least a handful of new strategies that will revolutionize how you do ministry. Remember, it's all about helping people take their next step toward Christ.

Fuel the Pioneering Spirit

I've talked with a lot of church leaders who have good memories of their early days in leadership. I've heard, "Everyone was pulling in the same direction," or "We knew we were going to accomplish something big." There was a sense that God was going to use them and that everyone was serving and contributing because there was so much to do. They were always looking forward to the next week to see what God was going to do.

I call it a "pioneering spirit." It must be similar to the spirit of the early pioneers who headed West. They saw the whole country before them, even when they weren't sure what was around the next mountain or through the next forest. They anticipated the adventures that might lie ahead.

Many times a church loses that pioneering spirit as it ages or "settles in." This can also happen when a church buys or builds a facility. People stop serving, excitement wanes, and complaining becomes more prevalent than vision casting.

I propose it does not have to be that way. It is possible to strategically build events or occasions into the life of the church that innately produce momentum and motivate involvement.

Here is what I suggest: Strategically plan churchwide events, campaigns, or projects at least every six months for the purpose of generating and maintaining momentum. If you do this every six months, the whole church will always be looking forward to something even as they remember and celebrate a positive event that happened within the past few months.

> Strategically plan church-wide events, campaigns, or projects at least every six months for the purpose of generating and maintaining momentum.

Here are some events that can create anticipation:
- groundbreaking celebrations
- the completion and opening of classrooms or buildings

- community outreach events
- new services or ministries
- hiring new staff members
- weekend series
- building campaigns

Plan. Write in "momentum builders" on the calendar every six months for the next two years. Dr. John C. Maxwell has taught church leaders much about momentum. He says in his book *The Maxwell Leadership Bible*: "Without momentum, even the simplest tasks can seem insurmountable. But with momentum on your side, the future looks bright, obstacles appear small, and trouble seems temporary. With enough momentum, nearly any kind of change is possible."

This one strategy will raise morale, build momentum for life change, involve more people in ministry, and grow your church at a pace that will surprise you.

—Tim

2 Good Leaders Let Good People Go

"Can two people walk together without agreeing on the direction?"
(Amos 3:3, New Living Translation)

There are times when the best decision is to release someone from a ministry or even from the church. These are the hardest conversations I've ever had. It's different in the corporate world. You can distance your emotions in those instances because "it's business." But when you are dealing with people in the church, the stakes are much higher. Sometimes letting someone go is what's best for the church. It's what's best for you. Most times it's also what's best for the person you're releasing.

> Sometimes letting someone go is what's best for the church.

As a leader, you will face these decisions. Some will involve staff. Others will involve key volunteer leaders. Both are very difficult. Leaders face these tough calls for a variety of reasons. In some instances, a staff member or volunteer has lost commitment to the vision. That happens. As people grow in their faith journeys, God frequently develops areas of passion that may or may not gel with the vision of your church. Thankfully, there are many great local churches. Most share the same ultimate goal of helping people meet Jesus and mature in their faith; however, each church has a unique DNA. The mission, vision, values, and strategy differ from church to church. This is what allows the global church to effectively reach all kinds of people. Over time it's not unusual for some people to begin to find that their hearts just don't beat fast for the particular direction your church is going. In those instances, you need to encourage those people to find another church where they can serve.

In other cases, people once had the gifts and abilities to serve your church, but your ministry has outgrown their abilities. These are hard conversations. not only have you worked together, you've also shared your lives. The fact is, though, it takes a very different set of skills to serve a church of a thousand than it does a church of two hundred. Granted, as a leader, one of your primary responsibilities is to help volunteers and staff develop their skills and abilities through ongoing training and mentoring. When a person's abilities can't keep pace with the demands of a particular position, you may need to help him or her find a better-fitting role. Sometimes that role will be within your ministry. Other times, it may have to be in another church.

Protecting the health of the church must come first.

The most challenging situation involves people who have ignored coaching about attitude or have begun to cause division within the church. Of course, these situations vary in their magnitude. not all instances justify separation. But there are times you must take immediate action to protect the integrity of your ministry. Sometimes people just need a swift kick in the pants to get back on track. Other times, healing and restoration can't begin until someone has been removed from a ministry role. In some instances, relational restoration isn't the primary need—protecting the health of the church must come first. It's why Matthew 18 teaches us that some people must also be removed from fellowship.

It's in situations like these that the church is relying on leaders to step up and be leaders. As difficult as it may be, don't shrink from it. God will provide wisdom, strength, and healing, but it's up to you to make the tough call.

—Tony

3 Count the Cost Before Hiring a Family Member

Consider these scenarios:

• A senior pastor meets with members of the board or personnel committee to convince them that the church needs a new children's ministry director. They agree but then don't know how to respond when he suggests that the most qualified person is his wife.

• A lay leader notices a staff person who is not getting the job done and is lazy, unethical, or incompetent. He believes the church leaders would want to know. The problem is that the staff person is the pastor's son.

• The finances are taking a nose dive, and the senior pastor must make a decision about staff layoffs. There are five staff members, and one of them is his wife. Who does he let go?

It is commonplace in churches for two or more individuals from the same family to be on staff. It's almost like a family business. Dad started the church, and Mom had a key staff position. Their son returns from college and joins the staff as an associate. Their nephew works on the maintenance staff, and their daughter-in-law works in children's ministries. Many times this arrangement is very successful. We've heard of thriving local churches in which a son's transition into senior leadership is flawless. However, we've also heard of train wrecks. One thing goes wrong, and suddenly a number of key staff members resign.

There are no biblical mandates regarding hiring family members. But we can learn from the tough experiences of others and be "wise as serpents" (Matthew 10:16, King James Version). There are several reasons you should count the cost before hiring a spouse or any other family member.

• **Some people will question your motives.** They will assume that you cannot be objective, and so your decisions will automatically be suspect.

• **You could lose objectivity.** It's possible to lose your ability to discern or make wise decisions about the church. You may excuse inaction, defend incompetence, hide immorality or unethical behavior, or shelter your spouse or relative from necessary accountability.

 • **You could put a strain on your family relationships.** Ministries change; interests change; responsibilities grow. There may be a time you have to make some difficult employment decisions. Jobs come and go. Families last a lifetime. Don't sacrifice peace in your home for a job.

If you do hire family members, decide in advance how their employment will be handled. Here are two guidelines we follow at Granger:

 • We will not hire the spouse of any Senior Management Team member. We do not want to put ourselves in the position of having to make difficult employment decisions about one of our spouses.

 • We will not hire a husband and wife to work in the same department. There may be a staff guy in the arts department and his wife in the children's ministries, but they are never in the same area.

Don't sacrifice peace in your home for a job.

We do our best to separate relationships from difficult staff decisions. This is hard and sometimes impractical, but we want to make decisions based on the merits of the situation, not on the relationships involved.

In some instances hiring a family member may be your best option, but make sure you count the cost before you take that step. Your church will appreciate it, and it will make sitting down for Thanksgiving dinners enjoyable for years to come.

—Tim

Flexibility Is a Higher Value Than "Flashy"

It was September 1998. We had designed a sloped-floor, state-of-the-art twelve-hundred-seat auditorium. It would have a performance stage, a "fly loft" for lighting and stage flats, a greenroom, incredible sightlines, and a hydraulic spiral lift that spanned two levels for moving equipment and stage sets up and down.

There was only one problem. We couldn't afford it. Oh, we could have figured out how to make it work. But we would have mortgaged our future. Why? Because it wasn't expandable. At that time, we were running nearly fifteen hundred in attendance, and we knew we'd be averaging over two thousand the day we moved into the completed space.

Our dream space would have allowed us about three years of growth, and then we'd be maxed out. The five thousand attending would absolutely love it, but there would be no room for our friends or lost neighbors. We'd be leveraged financially, and it would be many years before we could replace it with another auditorium.

Why? Because it wasn't flexible. It was cool. It was artsy. Someone even called it sexy. But it wasn't flexible.

So we threw away the blueprints and started over. This time, we designed and built a box. An expandable box. A beautiful, high-quality box. A box with great acoustics and tremendous sightlines and a wonderful stage. A flat-floor box that turned out to be the best decision we could have made.

We have grown from eighteen hundred to four thousand in the thirty months since the box opened. Our finances will allow us to expand the box in 2004. The expanded box (OK, really a rectangle after its expansion) will seat well over two thousand and will allow us to grow to ten thousand in multiple services before it's full.

Choosing to be flexible rather than flashy will enable us to reach thousands more people than we could have with our dream auditorium. There's nothing wrong with state of the art or bells and whistles. But if including them will sacrifice your future growth potential, you may want to reconsider.

—Tim

5 If It Feels Good, Check the Data

"The heart of the discerning acquires knowledge; the ears of the wise seek it out" (Proverbs 18:15).

It's decision time. As Christ followers, we have the benefit of the Holy Spirit to provide wisdom and guidance as we face choices. The danger exists, however, that we'll follow emotion rather than discernment as decisions come along. There's an appropriate place for emotions in decision making. We can't push them aside, but they shouldn't drive our decision making.

By the same token, decisions shouldn't be made strictly on a factual basis. If you rely totally on the numbers, you miss the faith factor. The challenge is to discern God's will as you try to appropriately balance facts and faith.

As you study the information available to discern God's will, I want to caution you against three analysis errors. These are instances when your emotions tell you things are good, when in reality things aren't as positive as you perceive them to be.

Error 1: Monitoring the wrong measures. Typically this error involves measuring activity rather than outcomes. Sometimes we mistake busyness for success. Just because your church calendar is completely full doesn't mean things are good. In this case, measuring the number of events or activities isn't as important as evaluating the outcomes. Through those events, have people taken steps in their spiritual journey? Are they more mature in their faith? It's easier to measure activity, so that's what we tend to focus on. We should be more interested, however, in the impact these activities are having on people's lives.

> The challenge is to discern God's will as you try to appropriately balance facts and faith.

Error 2: Ignoring cycles. Ministry happens in cycles. The school calendar, holidays, and seasons all affect the numbers. That's why it helps to analyze trends and comparisons from year to year. Having five hundred people at your weekend services in July, for example, may be far better than having six hundred people in December. Monitor increases for like-periods in the ministry cycle to determine if your church is growing or declining.

Error 3: Analyzing ministry in a vacuum. Here's a specific example. We recently learned that the number of people serving in leadership roles at our church has increased by 5 percent from the same period a year ago. The number of leaders is going up. Sounds positive, doesn't it? It is, until you consider the fact that our weekend attendance, membership, small-group participation, and ministry connections all increased by 40 percent over the same period. Red flags! Leadership growth isn't keeping pace with the rest of the ministry. As a result of that analysis, we know leadership recruitment and development should be a key focus for us in the coming months. It's a good reminder to consider the total health and balance of your church. Just because an area is experiencing growth doesn't necessarily mean things are going well.

Measure outcomes. Monitor cycles. Pay attention to balance. Use these three reminders to track progress and make better ministry decisions.

—Tony

6 Don't Spend Your Life With Your Critics

Have you ever met someone who had the gift of criticism? or the gift of whining? or the ability to see the negative in everything? Do you sometimes dread reading your comment cards or opening the mail? You wonder, "Who is complaining this week?" Or "I wonder what Ethel Snodgrass is upset about today?"

I used to think that I needed to take the time to convince every critical person to see things my way. I was also convinced that if I just talked to these folks long enough, I could change their thinking and they would feel better after we had finished talking.

I soon learned I was wrong. I was just wasting precious minutes God had given me to invest in meaningful and effective ministry.

Answering every criticism and explaining every questioned action will wear you out!

Answering every criticism and explaining every questioned action will wear you out! I'm convinced it will shorten your life, reduce your heart for people, and create a cynical spirit within you. You need to filter your critics. Here are some suggestions for doing this.

First, know your target. Who are you trying to reach? (Don't say, "The world." You should know exactly whom you are uniquely gifted to reach in your community). Next, determine whether the criticism is coming from your target. If it comes from people outside your target, affirm the value of the opinion, and free them to find a church in your community where they fit. If they are in your target, do what you can to help them understand the issue.

At Granger, the target of our weekend services is pre-Christians, specifically the unchurched. Yet the vast majority of criticism we receive comes from churchgoing people who have popped into our church for a few weeks or months and have decided they need to fix us. They come to us with preconceptions about how church is supposed to happen. This is "church baggage." When we don't fit their image, they criticize, whine, and tell us what we are doing wrong. Since they are not the target of our weekend services, we affirm them, tell them we love them, and say, "There are all kinds of churches for all kinds of people. There are probably dozens of churches in this community that you would be more comfortable attending."

However, if we receive criticism about our weekend service from our target, a pre-Christian who has started attending recently, we listen carefully. We try hard to understand the complaint. We want to design an experience that will reach these people and their friends, so we very much want to hear their feedback. I'm not talking about anything that would water down the gospel or change the message. It is about removing distractions so nonbelievers can open their hearts and hear more clearly. We often say around Granger that we are providing "a safe place for a dangerous message." It also gives us an opportunity to start a dialogue with these individuals that we hope will lead to their meeting Jesus.

It's OK to listen to criticism as long as you choose the right critics. Don't spend time and energy on people who aren't a part of your ministry target.

—Tim

7 Get Geeked About Gadgets

Everyone's expected to do more with less—more ministry with less staff, more ministry with less money, and more ministry with less time. One way to live with this reality is to make sure your team is properly equipped with the latest gadgets to encourage multitasking. I have no way to measure it, but I really believe I give more time to ministry and accomplish far more because I have the right tools at my fingertips. Is it twice as much? I don't know, but it's significant, and it's a relatively cheap return on investment when you consider the cost of salary and benefits that it would take to replace my time.

> I give more time to ministry and accomplish far more because I have the right tools at my fingertips.

Here are some tools to consider:

• **Laptop.** There are many functions and roles in which a desktop computer is appropriate, but others really require a laptop. Laptops allow freedom to discuss projects in off-site strategy sessions, message preparation from the home office, and easy-to-use presentation capabilities.

• **Cellphones and voice mail.** These are a must. They help you stay connected to your ministry leaders and to the church office while on the road.

• **Personal Digital Assistant (PDA).** Unless you expect all ministry to take place at the church, a PDA (such as a Palm Pilot or Pocket PC) is an efficient way to track appointments, tasks, and contacts while on the go.

• **Instant Messaging (IM).** Of course, e-mail is standard, but IM is the next tool that will change how we communicate with our teams. These real-time Internet conversations create opportunities for instant feedback and decisions without the delay of e-mail. In some companies, it's become one of the primary methods of communication. The point is that we need to continually evaluate how we're equipping our team members.

This includes equipping volunteers. For example, at Granger, we grew to thirty-five hundred people in attendance before we hired anyone to produce the videos used in our services. Until then, they were all created by volunteers. In some instances the church assisted these volunteers by purchasing computer equipment and software for home computers so the volunteers could more effectively fulfill their ministry roles. We don't do things like that for every volunteer who walks through our doors, but when someone is willing to give twenty hours or more each week to serve Jesus in a critical role, we'd be foolish not to make the right tools available.

Get geeked about gadgets. It's the cheapest way to add hours to your ministry team without adding staff.

—Tony

8 If Someone Hasn't Left Your Church Recently, Your Vision Is Probably Too Broad

"Imagine what would happen to a commercial radio station if it tried to appeal to everyone's taste in music. A station that alternated its format between classical, heavy metal, country, rap, reggae, and southern gospel would end up alienating everyone. No one would listen to that station!"

—Rick Warren, *The Purpose-Driven Church*

This analogy applies to most churches. You ask them, "Who is your target?" and they answer, "The world." You ask, "What is your mission as a church?" and they provide the standard response: "To glorify God."

That preaches well, but too often it produces an impotent church that is powerless to influence a community. If churches across America don't begin strategically targeting specific segments of our population, we risk losing ground in accomplishing the Great Commission!

> If churches across America don't begin strategically targeting specific segments of our population, we risk losing ground in accomplishing the Great Commission!

You may have heard a church leader say, "We pattern our church after the New Testament church." Really? Which one? The church at Ephesus? Corinth? Philadelphia? Smyrna? Pergamum? Thyatira? Sardus? Laodicea? There were many New Testament churches, and each one had a unique target audience that was based on culture, language, community size, and many other factors.

Here's what I would suggest for a church that's just starting or one that's going through a major change:

• **Start very focused.** Have a laser-targeted vision for your church as a whole, and then for each event or outreach as well. Who are you trying to reach with your weekend service? with your Web site? with your children's programs?

• **Do a few things well.** Don't try to be all things to all people. Figure out your core competencies, and knock the ball out of the park! Perhaps at first you can focus on children's ministry but not youth programs. Maybe you can focus on small groups but not singles ministry.

• **Add slowly.** Take on one major new outreach or ministry each year that helps you reach your target. For example, add a junior high program this year. Add high school next year. Raise up leaders, but don't launch ministries until you have identified a trained leader to run point.

Don't sweat it if people leave your church because you aren't meeting their specific needs. It's OK. Free them to go elsewhere. Say, "There are dozens of churches in this community, and you'll probably find what you're looking for somewhere else."

When someone leaves, it will hurt. That pain, however, may be because you are doing *exactly* what God wants you to be doing!

—Tim

Work Yourself Out of a Job

"Now look around among yourselves, brothers, and select seven men who are well respected and are full of the Holy Spirit and wisdom. We will put them in charge of this business. Then we can spend our time in prayer and preaching and teaching the word" (Acts 6:3-4, NLT).

Keep the tasks that add the most value, and give everything else away.

You're probably already familiar with this story in the book of Acts. The church was growing so fast that the leadership couldn't keep up with the preaching and teaching as well as the administrative responsibilities. As a result, some of the widows in the church were not getting appropriate care. The solution was to recruit seven believers to take over the food program so the church leaders could continue to focus on prayer, preaching, and teaching. In the end, the widows got their food in a more timely fashion, and the church was able to widen its influence in the community.

This is a critical lesson for you and your leadership team. Strive to give your jobs away. This is true for the volunteer leaders in your ministry as well as the senior pastor and the church board. Keep the tasks that add the most value, and give everything else away. This will allow you to focus on the priorities while giving others the chance to have a fulfilling ministry.

At Granger, we are constantly evaluating all that we do and looking for the people who are best wired to take over our current ministry roles. That frees us up to launch new ministries and handle the expanded leadership responsibilities of a growing church.

Taking these steps will enable you to successfully give your job away:

- Identify tasks others could do.
- Find individuals capable of handling them.

- Share your vision, and ask these people to fill the roles.
- Tell them how to do it.
- Show them how to do it.
- Have them show you how to do it.
- Monitor their progress.
- Celebrate their success.

Here's what we've learned: In almost every instance in which we've released ministry to lay people who have the abilities and passion for particular roles, the ministry takes a step forward. The church gains by finding people who are many times better gifted in a specific role, the lay people find a fit that brings them a sense of purpose and community, and the staff and volunteer leaders gain more time to focus on their primary ministry responsibilities. Everyone wins.

—Tony

10 Visit Other Churches and Steal Their Stuff

A friend of mine was a youth pastor in a church of about four hundred. We would occasionally talk on the phone to pass ideas back and forth. He was amazed by how often I spoke of getting new ideas from churches I visit. He said that his senior pastor didn't see any value in visiting other churches. "The Bible is God's revealed will, and if we stay in the Word, then we'll have all the ideas we need," the senior pastor would tell my friend.

We should continually be figuring out the best way to communicate the timeless message of the gospel.

How unfortunate. We are to be students of our ever-changing culture. We should continually be figuring out the best way to communicate the timeless message of the gospel. Tens of thousands of churches across the world are engaged in the same effort. Many of them have already figured out how to be effective in an area in which we are looking for answers! We may not be able to learn everything from one person, but we can all learn something from everyone.

The leaders at Granger have many times jumped into a car or a plane to visit a church that's hitting the ball out of the park in an area in which we need help. After visiting, we may think of a hundred things we'd never do because they don't fit in our setting. On the other hand, we might come away with two or three ideas that could revolutionize our ministry. Everywhere we go, we can learn something.

Here is a short list of ideas we've stolen from other churches:

• the Purpose-Driven Church model from Saddleback in Lake Forest, California (www.saddleback.com)

• dozens of great drama scripts from Willow Creek, near Chicago (www.willowcreek.com)

• a flexible auditorium design from Northwoods Community Church in Peoria, Illinois (www.nwoods.org)

• creative theming ideas for children's rooms from Church On The Move in Tulsa, Oklahoma (www.churchonthemove.net)

- great ideas for a youth building from Resurrection Life Church in Grandville, Michigan (www.reslife.org or www.getfloored.org)
- many weekend series ideas from Dr. David Foster at Bellevue Community Church in Nashville (www.hopepark.com)
- good ideas about advertising in the community and creatively using radio from Cedar Creek Community Church in Perrysburg, Ohio (www.aroundthecreek.com)
- a vision for a fish aquarium in the children's center from Lake Pointe Church, near Dallas (www.lakepointe.org)
- other ideas for services, ministries, and building design from scores of churches around the world

Of course, we use the word *stolen* sarcastically. If you quote from a message or book, you should always give credit to the author. If you reprint published material or copy a logo or graphic design, you must first get permission. I've never heard anyone from a church say, "No, you can't use it." Churches are typically honored to be asked. And, it goes without saying, if you quote from this book, you should mention that "never before has such brilliance been observed" or something along those lines.

—Tim

11 Maintain an Appropriate Span of Care

How many pastors have you watched run themselves ragged? They may seem to be the busiest people on the planet, but they don't seem to accomplish much. They are always meeting with someone, answering the phone, browsing e-mail, checking voice mail, or reading the mail. They are busy, busy, busy.

They might be subconscious victims of church growth. Here is what happens: The church is small. The pastor does virtually everything. He (or she) is personally responsible for the youth ministry, nursery, women's ministry, every weekend service, all the music, meeting with the elders, planning the annual events, and so on. He does it all. Then the church begins to grow. Unfortunately, he can't give anything up because his heart is in everything. Ultimately, he might be directly responsible for twenty-five different volunteer leaders.

That's way too many. He will begin losing track of details, his family will suffer, and the infrastructure of the church will implode because he hasn't learned to delegate leadership along with tasks.

> The ideal number of people to have in your span of care is six. Eight is OK. Ten is too many.

My opinion is that the ideal number of people to have in your span of care is six. Eight is OK. Ten is too many. Twelve or more is downright unhealthy and dangerous (OK, Jesus had twelve, but he was Jesus).

You are responsible for too many people if you
- don't have time to listen to them.
- don't have time to encourage them.
- don't have time to return their phone calls and e-mails.
- don't have time to pray for them.
- don't know their kids' and pets' names.

• don't have time in your schedule to meet with each of them on a regular basis (for some, that may be necessary daily; for others, weekly; and for others, twice a month).

• don't have time to talk about life, family, and hobbies because you're always talking "business."

This applies to the small groups, the staff, the leadership body, and every department. For example, in your children's ministry a volunteer leader should have no more than six to eight children in his or her span of care. If the number is greater than that, most volunteers will not be able to spend the right amount of time each week caring for, talking to, and praying for those children and their parents.

Everyone in your span of care needs you to give T.I.M.E. to them. That is, you should Touch, Inspire, Motivate, and Encourage each person on your team often. Decide today to delegate authority so you can lead with strength and health.

—Tim

12 Put a Couch in Your Women's Restroom

Many church leaders see a building that works well somewhere else, and they incorrectly think that it will be equally effective in their locale. However, every church deals with a different culture. You must design your building to fit your culture.

Let me give you an example from our experience. We've learned that women typically visit our church in advance of their husbands. We've found again and again that men are more skeptical of organized religion, and women often scout churches by themselves. The husband will say, "When you find one that works for you, I'll visit it with you."

We've also learned that women in Granger don't like waiting in line at the restroom. Yet in virtually every church building, as well as in many civic and public buildings, the women's restrooms are too small! There is often a line leading out into the hallway because someone didn't think far enough ahead to design appropriately sized restrooms. So at Granger, we designed according to our culture. We created a huge, beautifully decorated women's restroom that even has an area with a couch, lamp, and loveseat in it! We want the women who are visiting Granger for the first time to leave the women's restroom saying, "This is my church!" before they ever get to the auditorium.

Something else we've observed about the women in our culture is that either they are involved in careers and don't have time to cook, or they are stay-at-home moms who don't have the energy to cook every night for their families, let alone for others. So potlucks or carry-in meals don't work at Granger. Most women would rather contribute money than a prepared dish. At Granger, we designed our space according to our culture. Our kitchen is the size of the broom closet at most other churches. Why? Because anytime we offer food service, we have it catered.

Study your people, then design your building so that it works in your culture. That will help you reach your target, and it may also help you avoid overdosing on green bean casserole.

—Tim

Find Administrators With a Touch of "Artist" in Them

"The machines that are first invented to perform any particular movement are always the most complex, and succeeding artists generally discover that, with fewer wheels, with fewer principles of motion, than had originally been employed, the same effects may be more easily produced."

—Adam Smith, "The Principles Which Lead and Direct Philosophical Inquiries," sct. 4, *Essays on Philosophical Subjects*

When we think of artists, we tend to think only of those people who can sing, dance, act, or paint. In reality, your ministry needs an artist in every position, including the top administrative position. That administrator needs to be able to dream big dreams. He or she must love change. That person needs to be about embracing new vision. Your top administrator should have a touch of the artist in him or her.

There's a place in your organization for those who love policies and "maintaining," but your top administrator must be able to think outside the box. You need someone who can help create processes for how your ministry operates. You need someone who can develop and effectively manage change so systems are in place to make decisions and minister to people. You need someone who creates systems and then continually considers methods for improving those systems by removing barriers to growth. Growing churches require different types of organizational structures and systems. The same strategy that allows a church to grow from one hundred to three hundred will not allow a church to grow from one thousand to three thousand.

A church our size can't afford to wait for purchasing decisions from the finance committee, staffing decisions from the personnel committee, or ministry decisions from the education committee. We have systems in place to process these decisions with appropriate accountability established to monitor results. For example, each of our pastors and directors may make purchasing decisions up to $2,000 as long as the expenditures are included in their budgets. If a purchase exceeds that amount, the executive pastor must also approve payment. If it's an expenditure that will increase the overall church budget, the board must approve the change. With this system in place, ministry can move forward without unnecessary delays, and the board still has the overall responsibility for establishing spending priorities.

If your church is not growing, a critical question to ask is whether its current structure and systems are prohibiting growth. Your administrator needs to move beyond the current situation to consider how your church must change to maximize ministry success.

Let me provide a word of warning here. It's important to maintain an appropriate balance of creativity (chaos) and efficiency (order). If you begin to lean too heavily on creativity, everything will be constantly changing and nobody will know what's coming next. As a result, people will get frustrated and may withdraw from your ministry. Remember: For most people, change is not easy. On the other hand, if you focus only on efficiency, you'll become good at what you currently do, but you'll never change. Your ministry will eventually become irrelevant to the culture. A good administrator helps strike the right balance between order and chaos.

—Tony

14 Keep Influencers in the Loop With the Inside Scoop

We've all seen it happen. We're in a meeting, and the presentation has been made. An awkward silence ensues as we wait to see who will ask the first question. We're not sure yet which way the decision will go. Eventually, all heads turn toward her. She is the one from whom all others take their cue. It may stem from her tenure, wisdom, personality, or opinionated style—but there is no doubt she is the leader. She doesn't have a leadership title, and she's not sitting at the head of the table, but she is definitely the leader. If she's in favor of the proposal, it will pass. If she isn't, it will fail. End of story.

We call these people *influencers*. There is always at least one person who must be convinced before you can progress. It might be one teacher in your children's ministry planning group. It might be one member on your deacon or elder board. It might be one musician in your band.

> There is always at least one person who must be convinced before you can progress.

It's pretty easy to identify an influencer. As you meet with the members of your group, watch their eyes and their interactions. You'll see who in the group is respected, who is feared, and who will lead. You'll find your influencer.

Once you've identified the influencer, follow this rule that I learned from John Maxwell in a conference several years ago: "Don't skip the meeting before the meeting."

This one principle will help you so much. It's timeless. You'll never have enough tenure in a church or strong enough relationships with a congregation for this not to be true. Anytime you want to start something new, make a change, add a program, or expand the budget—make sure you don't skip the meeting before the meeting. Be sure to meet with every key influencer ahead of time. Ask influencers what they think, tell them you need their insight, and ask them what questions they have and what additional information they need.

By doing this, you'll accomplish several things:

• **You'll discover the holes in your presentation.** Influencers will ask questions you hadn't considered. You'll get a peek into the thinking of your team, and you'll know better how to process the change you are about to introduce.

• **You'll communicate to them that they are hugely valuable!** They'll feel and really believe that you care what they think and that you appreciate their opinions. They'll feel as if they have "inside information."

• **You'll get new ideas about implementing the change or launching the program.** Many times you'll walk away amazed that someone actually had an idea that was better than yours!

• **You'll prepare the influencers for your presentation.** They'll already be on board with you when everyone else looks to them for approval. Instead of risking an emotional response by surprising them with new information, you will see them responding in approval as you present the plan.

Follow this advice for quick and painless meetings. Don't surprise your influencers; be proactive by holding the meeting before the meeting.

—Tim

15 Never Launch a Ministry Without a Leader

How many times have you heard someone in your church suggest, sometimes strongly, that the church establish a new ministry? Maybe it's more community outreach. Maybe it's a new ministry for single parents or a ministry targeted to the next generation. These all seem like valid ministry initiatives for most churches; however, many times the people recommending them aren't also prepared to step up and lead.

There are many great ministries that may fit the mission and vision of your church. But if God hasn't also helped you identify a ministry leader, it's probably not the right time to launch. The ministry is going to end up on your plate whether you want it to or not, if you decide to launch prematurely. Unless you plan to remove another ministry function from your responsibilities—and that's a valid consideration—then you shouldn't commit to starting a program without first selecting a leader.

> You shouldn't commit to starting a program without first selecting a leader.

Whenever you determine that a new ministry fits the purposes of your church, you need to identify someone—and most often it's a layperson—to lead it. But you should select a leader only after you've identified someone on your management team, paid or unpaid, to oversee that new ministry initiative. At Granger, for example, every ministry is connected to one pastor on our Senior Management Team (SMT). If we were going to begin a divorce-recovery ministry, we'd identify one of the SMT pastors to oversee the effort, and we'd identify a staff or volunteer leader to run point on this new ministry.

Identifying leaders before you start new programs will also force you to focus on your church's primary purpose, to fulfill the Great Commission. For years at Granger, our primary focus has been reaching our community with the gospel message. We have developed the weekend services as our main vehicle for attracting a crowd and sharing the good news. With that in mind, we very quickly identified leaders and developed teams for music, drama, children's ministry, hospitality, and small groups. It's only been in recent years that we've added more specific ministry teams, particularly in the area of missions. It's not that we didn't want to send people to the missions field or to local outreach opportunities; we just knew we needed to focus our leadership horsepower on the weekend services first.

At Granger, we never launch a ministry without a leader. That means we're not only evaluating every ministry proposal to determine whether it fits our mission, vision, and values; we're also determining whether we have someone who can lead the ministry well.

—Tony

16 Don't Be Afraid to Bring in the Hired Guns

"Without wise leadership, a nation falls; with many counselors, there is safety" (Proverbs 11:14, NLT).

We tend to deceive ourselves. We think we have all the information needed. We overestimate our experience and knowledge. And we make mistakes. Our problem, of course, is that we lose perspective. You've heard the adage "Sometimes you can't see the forest because of the trees." Many times we're involved so deeply that we can't rise above the meetings, the events, and the people to see objectively.

Sometimes we need an individual from the outside to come in and lend perspective. We need someone who is able to walk in and see with "fresh eyes" things that we've never noticed. They can tell us what is working well and affirm the steps we've taken. They can also help us tweak systems and procedures. Many times we just need someone to say, "Don't give up!" At other times we need some of our key leaders to hear the "expert" legitimize seemingly radical change processes we've initiated.

> Sometimes we need an individual from the outside to come in and lend perspective.

We might need to hear about the mistakes others have made so we don't feel as if we're the only ones who ever try something that doesn't work. Wouldn't it be great if we could capitalize on the mistakes of others instead of making them ourselves? There are thousands of good people who have made some really colossal mistakes. It would be great to learn from them!

Here are some things to remember when you seek a consultant:

• **Ask for references.** Find out with whom they've consulted recently and talk to those leaders about affinity, results, style, and personality.

• **Don't expect profound new concepts.** A consultant many times will open your eyes to very basic ideas. You'll hear it and say, "Why didn't we think of that?" It's because the consultant views your situation with fresh eyes.

• **Objective affirmation is worth money.** At the end of the consultation, it's possible that the only thing said was "You're doing a great job. I've been to hundreds of churches, and you're hitting the ball out of the park. Keep it up! Don't quit!" If that's the only thing you, your staff, and your key leaders hear, it's worth a lot of money! That will give you and your people strength and stamina for the next phase of ministry!

• **Look for consultants who aren't consultants.** Your best consultants may not consider themselves to be consultants. A consultant may be the pastor of a church a little larger than yours. It may be a small-group director who is doing a phenomenal job of connecting people. It could be a children's leader who has a renowned ministry to families. Find out who is successful, call the person up, and say, "I'd like to buy one day of your time."

Remember the verse from Proverbs. When we don't have counsel, we fall. So avoid messing up by finding someone with fresh eyes to help you.

—Tim

Consultants We Have Found Helpful

• David Schmidt of J. David Schmidt and Associates (www.wiseplanning.net) helped us establish a vision statement for the next ten years.

• Tim Avery of INJOY Stewardship Services (www.injoystewardshipservices.com) customized a campaign that worked with our congregation and enabled us to raise nearly $4 million.

• Brett Eastman (www.lifetogether.com), formerly of Saddleback Church, gave us great ideas to help with our small groups.

• Tony LaBrosse of LaBrosse, Ltd. (www.labrosseltd.com) built the interactive elements of our new children's center.

Without Systems, All Decisions Rise to the Top

The irony of ministries that experience rapid growth is that the strengths that led to their initial successes may actually be detrimental to ongoing growth. In other words, it often takes a different set of talents and systems to maintain growth for the long haul. Ministries must trade a purely entrepreneurial instinct for an approach that also values management principles and systems.

Dave Ferrari, the founder of Argus Management Corporation, which specializes in turning around failing businesses, explained what leads to most business failures: "Ninety-five percent of the failures are due to internal problems. I can't tell you how many companies I've been to that have the fast-growing-company plaque on the wall and are about to go under. They don't have the systems and people in place" (from "Death by Unnatural Causes," by Stephanie L. Gruner, at www.inc.com).

Without systems, all decisions rise to the top. This is an important consideration as your ministry begins to bear fruit and the number of staff, lay leaders, and ministry programs grows. It may sound counterproductive for a church that's trying to remain on the cutting edge of creativity and innovation. And it's certainly a step away from how a church plant or the typical smaller church operates. In those situations, the senior pastor or administrative board does everything. These core leaders know about every strategic decision, every ministry team addition, and every purchase the church makes. This is helpful initially because it allows these leaders to establish the foundational mission, vision, and values that are critical for the ministry's long-term success.

But if the senior pastor or the administrative board holds on to all decision-making responsibilities, what once positively influenced the growth of the church can actually hinder continued growth when the church reaches a certain size. The answer to this problem is to create systems or policies that release decision-making responsibilities to the front lines of the ministry.

This concept is a stretch for some entrepreneurial leaders, because they try to avoid creating policies and procedures. They don't want anything to hinder the free flow of ideas and creativity. Unfortunately, without any guidelines for making even the simplest decisions, they all rise to the top of the organization. That will work for a while, but eventually it will stifle all creativity and innovation both on the front lines of ministry and at the senior leadership level. These people will spend all of their time making decisions on the biggest and smallest of issues. When everything including trivial matters rises to the top, ministry plateaus.

Here are some examples of policies or systems we've established at Granger to keep decisions from rising to the top:

• **Staff handbook.** This document outlines personnel issues such as employee benefits and leave-of-absence policies.

• **Purchasing policies.** These guidelines allow pastors and directors to make purchases up to $2,000 if the expenditures are included in the approved budget. Expenditures over that amount may be authorized by the executive pastor if they're already budgeted.

• **Staffing guidelines.** This document describes how staff leaders may recruit and select new employees after positions have been approved in the annual budget.

• **Facility scheduling process.** This Internet-based system empowers staff and volunteer leaders to reserve facility space for ministry programming and events.

Each of these systems has been put in place to push decision making to the front lines of our ministry. There are still guidelines that staff and volunteers must follow, but most day-to-day decisions can be made without having to wait for approval from the management team, the senior pastor, or the board.

Don't micromanage your church. Instead, create systems that release decision-making responsibilities. Empower the people on the front lines of your ministry.

—Tony

18 Buy the Farm... the Entire Farm

Land. It's limited. It's not a renewable resource. Money is different—you can always make more money. Even time is renewable. Every day, you get 1,440 new minutes to invest however you'd like. But land is limited. There is no way to create more land.

In 1986, Mark Beeson came to Granger, Indiana, to start a church. Just before the first services, a local businessman offered to give the church ten acres for a building site. At that time, there were no people yet. No building. The congregation hadn't even met for the first time. So imagine his surprise when Mark said, "Thank you very much, but that won't be enough land." The businessman, being much older and wiser, smiled at Mark's enthusiasm and misguided optimism. He had never personally seen a church with ten acres, so he was amused by Mark's idea that this church would need more. The man went ahead and donated the land to the church. Mark accepted the land for the church since there were still scores of adjacent acres that could be purchased later.

Mark understood the principle of buying the farm. He knew that land could always be sold later, but it may not be available for purchase later. What if we believe God will use this church to influence our community? What if thousands come to Christ? What if we experience revival? How big is our dream?

Six years later we purchased thirty acres in the heart of our area's growth corridor. It cost the church $6,000 per acre—a total of $180,000. A few years after that, we purchased an adjacent seven acres. By then, however, the cost was $62,000 per acre—a price tag of $434,000. Just recently, we purchased an additional fifteen acres that is also adjacent to us. But land values continue to climb, and this time the land cost the church $100,000 per acre.

If you have a dream, then share it with the church and buy as much land as you can. It will probably never be less expensive. Remember, it can always be sold later. (By the way, those original ten acres were sold to help fund a new building.)

—Tim

19 Staff Ahead of the Growth

It's the old chicken-and-egg quandary. Do you wait for fifty high school students to show up before you hire a youth pastor, or should you hire a youth pastor to attract fifty high school students? These are the discussion items on the church board agenda that leave everyone "scrambled" and "fried." You're just not sure what comes first.

Here's something I've noticed about churches. I've never seen a vibrant youth ministry without at least one person with a passion for students. I've never seen quality worship without at least one gifted worship leader. I've never seen small groups multiply or Sunday school programs increase without at least one faithful shepherd communicating the vision for biblical community. For ministry to expand, you need to staff ahead of growth.

Sometimes you need to hire someone to fill a glaring vacancy, but many times you should hire a person you don't need yet. Good leaders identify opportunities and threats before others see them. They know what's required to take the next mountain before others even recognize there's a new summit to reach. Because of that, it shouldn't be surprising if you add a staff position that others in your church don't believe is necessary.

At Granger, this strategy has been used since the church began. Even before the first service was held in 1986, the church had not one but two people on staff. Before we launched our first building project, we hired Tim to oversee the stewardship campaigns and construction. Before we started our new weekend service targeted to Gen X, we hired someone who knew the music style appropriate for that crowd.

> You don't necessarily have to pay someone to staff ahead of growth.

But you don't necessarily have to pay someone to staff ahead of growth. We frequently identify "volunteer staff" to lead ministry areas. It's one of the reasons Granger's staffing ratios are so low compared to other churches. Right now we have volunteers leading critical ministry areas throughout our church, including First Impressions (traffic, greeters, ushers, hospitality), hospital visitation, prayer teams, singles ministry, and drama. Of course, it's not uncommon for proven volunteer leaders to join our paid staff as our ministry needs continue to grow. (We discuss this in greater detail in Chapter 41, "Your New Staff Member Already Attends Your Church.")

I'm still not sure if the chicken or the egg came first. This, however, I do know—you can't count your chickens *or* your youth group members before they hatch. Remember to staff ahead of growth to multiply your ministry and to avoid getting egg on your face.

Now with that behind us, do you want to know why the chicken crossed the road?

—Tony

In November 2002, Granger had one staff member for every one hundred people in weekend attendance. According to a recent survey by the National Association of Church Business Administration (www.nacba.net), these are the averages by weekend attendance:

- Attendance of 0 to 299 = 1 employee for every 31 people.
- Attendance of 300 to 699 = 1 employee for every 36 people.
- Attendance of 700 to 1,499 = 1 employee for every 41 people.
- Attendance over 1,500 = 1 employee for every 46 people.
- Granger average 3,800 = 1 employee for every 100 people.

20 Be Clear. Be Specific. Write It Down.

"I don't know who I'm supposed to make happy."

"No one has any idea who is in charge."

"I'm confused. One day it seems as if the senior pastor is in charge. The next day it's the elder board. Then it's the executive pastor. Can someone tell me who I'm supposed to please?"

These are actual statements I've heard recently from friends in ministry. Good people are hired in important roles but then left to wonder how their success is measured. "How do I know if I've hit the ball out of the park or if I've sorely disappointed everyone?"

> Good people are hired in important roles but then left to wonder how their success is measured.

I recently spoke with a staff member at a church with several thousand attending each weekend. Their church conducted an inventory of staff and job descriptions and found a number of staff members who had no written job descriptions, no identifiable roles, and, in a few cases, no one to whom they were accountable. They asked, "Who is your boss? Who do you report to?" And the answer came back, "No one." Incredible!

If you want to make ministry a joy and delight for your pastors, then consider these simple suggestions.

Senior Pastor

Determine what's important. Provide your pastor with a short list of what you need from him or her. Once the church grows to 150 or 200 in size, you will begin adding staff. Your senior pastor needs to know what the leadership board expects him or her to continue doing. There are certain things that you don't want the senior pastor to hire someone else to do. Figure out what those things are, and agree upon them together. Here is an example.

The Five Things the Senior Pastor Must Do

1. Be the primary communicator at our weekend services.
2. Capture, carry, and communicate the vision for our future to the congregation.
3. Be faithful to his or her spouse and family.
4. Train leaders and hire staff to equip the saints for ministry.
5. Maintain personal integrity and holiness.

Then, as the budget allows, help your pastor hire others to accomplish what isn't on the list.

Other Pastors or Staff Members

• **Write it down.** Make sure they know exactly what you've hired them to do and what success in that job looks like.

• **One boss is enough.** Although you may use a group to interview potential staff members, once they accept don't ask them to report to a committee or an elder board. A youth pastor needs to keep one person happy. He or she shouldn't have to be concerned about an elder who is standing in the back of the room during a high school meeting. A music pastor needs to report to one person. He or she doesn't need to be concerned because a deacon said the music was too loud.

If you clearly write down expectations, you will free your pastors and staff to soar in their roles. Rather than wonder, they will know what it takes to be successful in their ministries.

—Tim

Good Stewardship Begins With Good Stewards

"For the love of money is a source of all kinds of evil. Some have been so eager to have it that they have wandered away from the faith and have broken their hearts with many sorrows" (1 Timothy 6:10, Today's English Version).

This will not be a surprise to you, but most people attending your church don't give to your ministry. In fact, the last time I checked, just over half the families in our church database had not contributed a dime. That percentage is likely a little higher for our ministry than most churches because we target people who are unchurched, but it's a reality that we deal with constantly. Obviously, this is primarily a spiritual development matter. People aren't going to give until Christ is at the center of their lives and they understand their resources are a gift from God to be used for his purposes.

> People aren't going to give until Christ is at the center of their lives.

Even with that in mind, there are many people whose financial hands are tied. Even if they wanted to honor God with their money, they can't because their finances are controlling their lives. It's for this reason that you need to be very intentional about developing a ministry to help people become good stewards of their financial resources.

There are probably gifted people in your church who could provide biblical teaching, counseling, and leadership for families who have their backs up against the wall financially. Your church should have an active ministry that includes opportunities for people to step into classes, small groups, and counseling relationships to address money problems. Again, you don't need to start from scratch. The Willow Creek Association (www.willowcreek.com) offers a number of resources from its Good Sense Ministry to help your church. Crown Financial Ministries (www.crown.org) also has many tools to equip people with biblical financial principles.

As you develop this ministry area, a handful of basics deserves your focus.

• **Budgeting.** People need to learn how to develop a spending plan to make sure their expenditures don't exceed their incomes.

• **Debt reduction.** You can show people how to get out of debt, particularly consumer debt, and get their money working for them through saving and investing.

• **Tracking spending.** Through the use of computer software packages or by simply tracking expenditures on paper, help people learn to monitor how they use their money.

• **Giving.** We teach the "10/10/80 Rule" at Granger: The first 10 percent should be invested back in God's kingdom. The second 10 percent should go into savings, and the remaining 80 percent is what you live on. We firmly believe that the spiritual discipline of stewardship is the foundation for financial discipline in all other areas.

You can be sure that most people aren't learning these basic skills anywhere else. Everything in our culture is encouraging people to spend money they don't have. Because of that, your church needs to help people experience financial freedom in their lives by establishing an active care ministry based on biblical financial principles.

—Tony

22 Somebody Has to Live and Die for the Database

If your church's goal is true life change in the lives of individuals and families, then an effective database may be one of your most important tools. Having correct information about the people in your ministry and the steps they are taking is absolutely critical.

For years at Granger, we had a hodgepodge of computer tracking systems including multiple databases and spreadsheets. Almost every ministry had its own tracking system, and there was no way to centrally monitor spiritual steps people were taking into small groups, classes, ministry, and giving. Simple things like address changes became troublesome because each ministry team had its own list. People became frustrated because it took several calls to simply get mail going to the right address. Now, with the need to track fifteen thousand people who are connected to our church in one way or another, we have to be strategic in how we track this critical information.

Here are some principles to follow:

Choose a staff person or volunteer to be your "database czar." In other words, someone has to live and die for the database. This person's job is to find the right software, train those who will be using it, and protect the data with vigor and passion. Such people have personalities that are cordial but firm. They are focused on details and aggressive in their style. They are trainers who don't just teach the lesson; they also stay with it until students understand.

Make decisions about what should be measured. You've heard the axiom "What gets measured gets done." Determine what you want to track. This is driven by your goals, your mission, and your vision. Once you know what you are trying to accomplish as a church, it will be simple to determine what needs to be measured. These things will tell you if you are making progress toward your vision or not. Here are some things we track at Granger:

• attendance

- giving
- small group involvement
- attendance at our four core classes (101, 201, 301, and 401)
- key spiritual steps
- areas in which individuals are serving

Protect the integrity of the information. Do this by limiting who can add, modify, or delete information. Only those who are trained and have apprenticed for a period of time should make changes. If untrained or poorly trained people are permitted to make changes, your data will become muddy. Phone numbers will be wrong, names will be misspelled, and other key information will be incorrect. When that happens, you no longer have any data you can trust, and it will take a monumental effort to dig your way out.

Back up your database. It is one of your most important assets. Back up the data regularly, and keep a copy off-site. Many organizations do this by keeping a different backup set for every day of the week (Monday through Friday), and always taking Friday's set off-site. This means that if the building burns down, your database will be no more than six days outdated.

With an effective database, you will make better decisions, your communication can be targeted, you'll know if your ministry is effective, you will be more personal in your conversations, you'll learn of spiritual weaknesses in your congregation, and you can track progress over time.

Pay attention to the database, and you'll be secure in what it is telling you. Don't pay attention to it, and soon it will be unreliable and worthless.

—Tim and Tony

23 Let Your Leaders Lead

"Obey your leaders and submit to their authority. They keep watch over you as men who must give an account. Obey them so that their work will be a joy, not a burden, for that would be of no advantage to you" (Hebrews 13:17).

There comes a time in growing churches when the leadership and administrative responsibilities exceed what lay people can accomplish in part-time, volunteer roles. When that occurs, your church needs to shift from a lay-led or committee-led ministry to one that allows the staff to lead. We at Granger made the shift when we were averaging about three hundred in weekend attendance.

The most effective arrangement allows for the staff to lead the day-to-day operations and implement ministry programming. The leadership board should make significant ministry decisions—such as budget approval, land purchases, building construction, and major contracts—and focus its prayer and energy on protecting the vision and values of the church.

> The most effective arrangement allows for the staff to lead the day-to-day operations and implement ministry programming.

Additionally, the number and scope of congregational votes should be limited. At Granger, for example, the only congregational votes we take are to approve the members of our board of directors, any annual reports required by our denomination, and major building projects.

We've created a Senior Management Team (SMT) to meet the day-to-day leadership responsibilities within our ministry. The SMT is composed of the senior pastor and other pastors or individuals selected by the senior pastor. Currently it includes the executive pastor, the pastor of creative arts, the pastor of connections, the pastor of life development, and the pastor of administrative services. Together, these people manage and operate the church. They are responsible for preparing the annual budget and ministry plan that are presented to the board. The SMT is responsible for daily oversight of staff and finances.

Every member of the SMT champions one or two key components of our ministry strategy. The pastor of connections, for example, is responsible for all the ministries in our church that connect people with membership and ministry. The pastor of creative arts is responsible for worship ministries, including the creation of compelling presentations in our weekend services that prepare hearts for hearing the message. Likewise, every ministry in our church is connected to one of the people on this leadership team. When we start a new ministry initiative, somebody on the SMT becomes responsible for spiritual and administrative leadership in that area.

Though this won't be the case in every church, members of the SMT also serve as elders for our ministry. We believe passages such as Acts 20; 1 Timothy 5; and I Peter 5 make no distinction between the roles of pastor and elder. With that in mind, the SMT is also charged with the responsibility of handling matters of church discipline.

The key to success in this staff-led arrangement is to find people with the leadership ability not only to oversee their specific ministry areas but also to ultimately have a passion and vision for the entire ministry.

By giving responsibility to this staff team, the leadership board does not give up its responsibility for accountability. Checks and balances are appropriate; however, the SMT must have the freedom to make routine day-to-day decisions with as little bureaucracy as possible. Ultimately, the board must still retain tight control over the mission, vision, and values, but the SMT must also have the authority to deploy resources and implement strategies. The church needs to let the leaders lead.

—Tony

24 You Can Pick Only Two

Size. Quality. Cost.

When dreaming about a new church building or addition, nearly everyone I've talked to says the same thing. "We need as much *space* as we can get at the highest *quality* at the smallest *price.*"

> Size, quality, and cost are the three primary values to consider when designing a building.

Size, quality, and cost are the three primary values to consider when designing a building. Most of us would like to control all three. However, you can pick only two, and the two that you pick are driven by your values.

For example, consider this scenario. Your church is four years old. You've been meeting in a school auditorium that seats 350 people for the past two years. The auditorium is very new and has comfortable chairs, great sightlines, and wonderful acoustics. Your attendance is averaging six hundred people in two services, but you are quickly growing and would like to build a facility that will accommodate more people in each service. You have the land and are ready to begin designing your first auditorium.

You will need to tell your architect which two values are most important to you. The architect will then be in control of the third choice.

• *You pick size and quality by stating,* "The new building must seat a minimum of five hundred people, and the level of quality must be the same as the school auditorium."

Then the architect will say, "A building of that size and at that level of quality will cost you this much money." It may be more money than you have, but you picked size and quality, so you can't control the cost.

• *You pick size and cost by deciding,* "It must seat a minimum of five hundred people, and we have only $600,000."

Then the architect will say, "In order to seat five hundred people for $600,000, we will have to alter some of the construction materials and methods." You can't control the quality. It is dictated by your choices.

• *You pick quality and cost by concluding,* "We have $600,000 for the new auditorium, and the level of quality must be the same as the school auditorium."

Then the architect will say, "In order to maintain the quality you would like for the money you have available, the new auditorium will be able to seat only three hundred people." You would like it to be bigger, but you are not able to control the size since quality and cost are higher values to you.

There are no right answers. I've seen successful churches make different choices. You may even make one set of choices for one project and a different set for the next project.

At Granger, we have chosen quality and cost on each of our four building phases. We have always been committed to financial responsibility, so cost has been a primary value. In addition, quality has generally won out over size in order to reach our specific target.

Your choice will be driven by your culture, your target, your leaders, your growth history, your growth potential, and your financial philosophy.

Decide in advance. Before you hire an architect, meet with your team and discuss your values.

—Tim

25 Nothing Is Certain Except Death, Taxes, and Building Campaigns

We launched our first building campaign in 1992. At the time, there were only three hundred people in the church. Since then, we've had consecutive campaigns beginning in 1995, 1998, and 2001. If yours is a growing church, then you'll be doing building campaigns forever. It really needs to become part of your culture. If you intend to reach more people for Jesus, it's going to take financial resources to expand your existing campus or to launch satellite locations or new church plants.

> You don't have to be afraid of launching your first campaign because there are many resources available to walk you through this process.

As with most ministry experiences, you don't have to be afraid of launching your first campaign because there are many resources available to walk you through this process. Rick Warren, for example, offers the "Time to Build Campaign Kit" through www.pastors.com. The kit includes sample computer files, sermons, brochures, and commitment cards, among other things, to assist you and your church leadership team.

There are also a number of companies that specialize in assisting churches during stewardship campaigns. Two companies that have assisted hundreds of churches through this process are INJOY Stewardship Services (www.injoy.com) and Resource Services, Inc. (www.rsi-ketchum.com). Though firms like these charge a fee for their services, their expertise will usually help you exceed what you may have been able to accomplish on your own. You may also want to check with your denominational leaders to find out what resources they have.

We've learned that, in addition to developing financial resources to fund ministry growth, there are several other benefits to building campaigns. In many respects, these benefits outweigh even the financial commitments and contributions God will provide. Here are some examples:

- **Vision.** God has given you a vision for the impact the local church can have. Stewardship campaigns offer a wonderful opportunity to recast that vision for how the church can expand its role in fulfilling the Great Commission. When people fully grasp what God has in store for your church, they'll feel honored and compelled to help support the project.

- **Teams.** A building campaign will not be successful without involving many people in prayer, events, communications, and a variety of administrative tasks. These offer opportunities to build teams and involve people in the process. Our last campaign included several hundred volunteers. Once people agree to serve during the campaign, in most instances they will want to continue serving. You'll also have a chance to identify and develop new leaders through this process.

- **Stewardship.** Campaigns offer the opportunity to teach your congregation about biblical stewardship principles. Before asking people to make a building pledge, we always teach that this commitment is in addition to their regular tithes and offerings. Many times people have committed for the very first time to make regular, sacrificial gifts to God's ministry through the teaching that's a part of any stewardship campaign.

Money should not be an obstacle to growth in your church. Stewardship campaigns offer a way to turn hearts toward God and help people learn the biblical principles of sacrificial giving.

—Tony

26 Perception Matters

It's not about trust.

It's not necessarily about strengths and weaknesses.

It's not even about your vulnerability to certain sins.

It *is* about perception. It *is* about what people think. Perception is reality. It may not be your reality, and it may not even be true. The fact is, it's reality for someone. The perception of how things appear, how they happened, or what was heard is everything. Perception matters.

> Our mission is too crucial and our message too important to let our ministry be sidelined for a week or a year by accusations based on perception.

Our mission is too crucial and our message too important to let our ministry be sidelined for a week or a year by accusations based on perception. As Jack Welch, former CEO of General Electric, said recently when he received criticism regarding his retirement package, "One thing I learned during my years as CEO is that perception matters. And in these times when public confidence and trust have been shaken, I've learned the hard way that perception matters more than ever" (quoted at www.money.cnn.com, September 16, 2002).

He was saying that it doesn't necessarily matter what is true. What really matters is what people *think* is true.

You must set up boundaries that protect you from the perception of wrongdoing. Here are some examples that we have implemented at Granger:

• No pastor or staff member will meet with a person of the opposite sex in a room that is closed from view. Why? Because perception matters. Every office and meeting room has windows in its door or walls so that it is visible from the hallway. This discourages people from saying that a sexual advance was made during a meeting.

• No married pastor or married staff member will ride in a car alone with a person of the opposite sex or meet him or her alone at a restaurant. Why? Because perception matters.

• No married pastor or married staff member will travel alone with a person of the opposite sex for any reason. Why? Because perception matters.

• No married pastor or married staff member will visit a person of the opposite sex in his or her home alone. It will never happen. Why? Because perception matters.

• No one counts money alone.

• No one who cuts checks is authorized to sign checks. No one who signs checks is authorized to cut checks.

Don't be legalistic, but limit your freedom just a little so that the cause of Christ is not hindered in your community of believers.

Why? Because perception matters.

—Tim

27 Use More Bytes and Less Paper

You traditionalists in the crowd aren't going to like this one. The tree huggers, on the other hand, may hail me as their poster boy. Of course, that would require cutting down a tree to make the poster paper, so maybe they won't like me either. I'm talking about replacing print communications with electronic communications. I just read an article (through an e-newsletter) indicating that Saddleback Church has replaced its weekly bulletin with an e-mail version. Can church be church without the weekly bulletin?

> Can church be church without the weekly bulletin?

The way people get news and information is shifting. According to statistics from the newspaper Association of America, over 80 percent of the population read a daily newspaper in 1964. Readership has steadily declined through the years, and in 2001 average weekday readership was only 54 percent. Instead, people are turning to the Internet for news. Even newspapers are turning to the Web. A study by The Media Audit, for example, found the Washington Post attracted over 40 percent of adults within its immediate market to its Web site. Of the eighty-five metro markets surveyed in 2001, twenty-eight daily newspaper Web sites attracted more than 20 percent of the adults in their immediate markets. That was up from only seven newspaper Web sites the previous year.

It's no surprise that more and more people are getting online. The data from a spring 2002 Harris Poll indicated that two-thirds of all adults in the United States are connected to the Internet. That shift in culture should also drive your communications strategy. Churches today should be moving resources from print communications to electronic communications. For the time being, print pieces will continue to complement electronic communications, but you should be implementing a strategy that gets information to people using the Internet. More and more of your people will prefer to receive information about your ministry electronically.

You can use a variety of methods to get information out to the masses, including your Web site, electronic e-mail lists (listservs), and weblogs—the equivalent of an online journal (see www.blogger.com). These methods can provide instantaneous information to thousands of people at a time. Ironically, the same people who you practically have to beg to read the bulletin

> The same people who you practically have to beg to read the bulletin announcements crave hearing those energizing words, "You've got mail."

announcements crave hearing those energizing words, "You've got mail." Once they read about the cool stuff that's happening, they can easily forward that message to friends and family members. These communications become relational methods for people to invite others to connect with your church.

The problem with almost every printed communication, including well-crafted prose like that found in this book, is that it becomes dated as soon as the ink hits the paper. With e-mail, on the other hand, you can push the latest details to everyone on your list on Friday morning as people are planning their weekends. The other added benefit is the cost. It's significantly cheaper to send e-mail messages than it is to print newsletters.

Stop the presses! It's time to click the "send" button.

—Tony

Feed Your Construction Workers a Hot Lunch

Take care of your construction workers. Talk to them every day. Find out about their families and their kids and their hobbies. Call them by name. Greet them every day. Introduce them to your friends and church members. Make them feel special. Let them know you care about them for *who* they are, not just for *what* they do.

At Granger, we've completed four major construction phases. Every time, our small groups have fed our construction workers once a week. During our first phase, we prepared a meal every Wednesday. The work crews could count on it. We set up sawhorses and plywood and served pizza, chili, or sloppy joes. Every week, a different small group volunteered to bring in the meal. The small-group members sat down with the workers and ate the meal with them.

The word got around. Other construction companies heard about it. In our second phase, many workers clamored to be assigned to our project. They heard about the love and generosity at Granger and wanted to be a part of that experience.

The driving purpose is totally selfless. We want to bless these people and love on them. We want to develop relationships with them. We want them to desire to attend a weekend service and hear about Jesus. If, down the road, they are going through a tough time, we want them to think, "I bet I could get some help from the people at Granger." We want them, some for the first time ever, to experience the love of Christ in a way that is tangible and real.

However, there is a huge side benefit to serving lunch to the workers. The quality of the work they do goes way up! It's not "just another job" to them. It's not just a project. They are now working on a building for Tim, Tony, Melanie, Kristin, and several other new *friends*. They begin to care about the building because they know and like us. They really believe that we care about them, and they want to do a good job for us.

So provide your construction workers with a hot lunch. Everyone will be fed and happy, and the benefits of a simple meal will be immeasurable.

—Tim

Disgruntled Secretaries Drain Dynamic Leaders

"Your attitude should be the same that Christ Jesus had" (Philippians 2:5, NLT).

Do some of the people in your life need an attitude adjustment? If those people are acquaintances, you can try to avoid them. If they're on the fringe of your ministry, you may need to encourage them. If they're in your family, you might just have to live with them. But if they're on your payroll, you get to decide what kind of attitude they have. That's right. You get to help decide whether someone has a good attitude. You should never pay for someone to be negative, disgruntled, or difficult to be with. People can do that in your life for free.

You get to choose what kind of attitudes your staff and volunteer leaders have. It's no different than expecting them to have moral integrity, a disciplined faith, and appropriate competencies to handle their particular roles. You should also expect these key people to be positive, encouraging, and fun. You should love spending time with them. And if they aren't "playing nice," you get to decide how long they stay before they have to find another sandbox to play in.

> If they're on your payroll, you get to decide what kind of attitude they have.

This is particularly critical with secretaries or administrative assistants. You're not only working with them; they become an extension of who you are. So if your assistant is moody and irritable, people begin to associate these negative characteristics with *your* leadership style. Yikes! Be grateful that you're allowed to divorce your assistant (unless, of course, you failed to follow our advice about hiring a spouse).

Surround yourself with people you like and who like you. Find people with a good sense of humor. Find attractive personalities. If you start hiring people who are fun to be with, you'll also notice more people wanting to hang around your church. Positive, encouraging people are magnets for drawing a crowd, and good attitudes breed good attitudes.

By the way, this same principle works with your kids. For example, "disgruntled daughters drain dynamic dads." While you're still bigger than your kids, you have a great opportunity to help them become better future employees, spouses, and servants for Christ by expecting good attitudes in addition to good behavior.

Don't ignore how people around you behave and interact. You have a chance to determine the personality of your church, and it begins with your leadership expectations. Help your team take on the attitude of Christ Jesus.

—Tony

30 Identify Leaders of Leaders, and Then Let Them Soar

"But in addition, you should choose some capable men and appoint them as leaders of the people: leaders of thousands, hundreds, fifties, and tens. They must be God-fearing men who can be trusted and who cannot be bribed" (Exodus 18:21, TEV).

Did you realize there are three types of people in your church? I know, you're probably saying, "Only three?" In this case, I'm referring to leadership capacity. Let me briefly describe who's in your church:

Doers. These are the people whose primary ministry function is completing a particular task or role. They are the servants who make things happen. They are the ushers, vocalists, nursery workers, small-group participants, and bulletin stuffers. They love to serve and are comfortable knowing they'll never have to call the shots. They just want someone to tell them what to do, and they'll do it.

Leaders of others. These are the Sunday school teachers, small-group leaders, and drama directors. They lead the doers. They help people complete specific ministry tasks. These people take responsibility for the spiritual development of their small flocks. They understand that ministry involves serving and sharing life with a small community of believers.

Leaders of leaders. These are the folks who can clearly communicate vision and have the leadership capacity to influence many people, including other leaders. They can be trusted to take on significant ministry roles within the church. These are the people who are sold on your mission, have demonstrated the ability to lead, can effectively communicate the vision, and can delegate the tasks.

One of your continuing roles as a pastor or ministry leader is to identify and call out people to one of these three roles. In reality, the church typically does a relatively good job of finding doers and leaders of others but fails to identify and equip leaders of leaders. The temptation is to believe that you have to pay someone for that role of leadership. The fact is, people in your church are ready to lead leaders. They just haven't been asked. And once you ask, you can equip them, train them, mentor them, and encourage them. Leaders need leading.

At Granger, we ask people to become leaders of leaders only if they have gone through each of our core classes and demonstrated the ability to lead. This ensures that they've met these minimum qualifications:

- They are Christ followers pursuing spiritual maturity.
- They are committed to the mission, vision, and values of our church.
- They are supporting the ministry with their prayers, their time, and their financial resources.
- God has wired them for a leadership role.

When trying to identify leaders of leaders, consider the people in your church who have demonstrated success in the business world. You may need to disciple them to encourage their spiritual development, but the fact that they've experienced success in the business world most likely means they are gifted leaders. Unfortunately, the church has historically done a poor job of tapping these resources. In many instances, successful businesspeople feel that the church is not a place that would use their skills. And then we turn around and try to fit them into existing ministries. Every servant and every ministry has value, but some people have leadership capacity that could better be used outside the nursery, the usher team, or the church choir. You need to steward your leadership resources as much as you do your financial resources by giving gifted leaders *real* leadership roles.

You'll never have enough staff to keep ahead of the growth in your ministry. Part of your role is to identify people for every ministry role God has for your church. This includes finding your most capable leaders.

—Tony

Send Your Bankers Audit Reports and Birthday Cards Every Year

Unless you elect to wait until you have cash on hand to fund building construction, the success of your project begins with the relationship you establish with a bank. Though there is nothing in the Bible that prohibits borrowing money, there are a number of passages about the importance of repaying loans. Because of that, it's critical that churches develop relationships with banks early in the planning process. This ensures the building project does not exceed the financial resources available to pay for the construction and confirms the church's ability to repay any debt.

Before you get too deep into planning your project, you should begin talking with a handful of banks to determine how much money will be available to fund the construction. You may want to contact local banks. Additionally, I would recommend talking to a bank that specializes in church loans. Begin the process by requesting proposals from several institutions. Typically the banks will want to see financial statements and attendance information from the past three years. They'll want to see giving records of your top contributors to make sure there is a balanced base to your financial position. Include a description of the project, detailing estimated costs for land purchase, site work, architectural fees, soft costs (such as furniture and equipment), and hard costs (construction expenses). Additionally, you should take this opportunity to tell the bank about your church's history, vision, and strategy. Begin to build a relationship with your bank. This will help both you and the bank make better decisions about your ability to borrow and repay loans.

Once you've received the initial proposals in writing, take time to interview the banks just as you would a potential staff member. This is also a good time to ask questions about the process. Borrowing money is a significant decision. You should enter into that type of decision only if you completely understand the commitments you are making. Talk to

> Make sure that your prospective bank has a good track record working with other churches.

the banks. Get to know their staffs. Find out if they've worked with other churches. Talk to those churches that are similar in size and ministry strategy to find out whether the relationships have been positive. There are many nuances to church ministry that make these transactions very different from a typical commercial loan, so make sure that your prospective bank has a good track record working with other churches.

Finally, make sure you consider the future when you enter into any banking relationship. If your church is growing, there will very likely be additional facility expansions. You need a banking relationship that can grow with the church. And, as in any relationship, there must be ongoing communication for those ties to remain solid. Keep your bank posted on how you're doing. It may not be necessary to send birthday cards, but your bank should know how God is using your ministry to influence your community.

—Tony

32 You Can't Fire Volunteers When the Construction Project Stalls

Many times churches place too much emphasis on *availability* and not enough emphasis on *ability*. This may be the primary mistake I hear when I talk with church leaders about their building projects.

It's not an intentional mistake. In fact, it comes from pure motives. Members of the church are excited about the growth of the church and are eager to volunteer their skills in areas in which they have interest, training, or expertise. The church leaders are excited about saving money on the project. They enlist available volunteers without appropriate reference checks, written agreements, or accountability systems, and then they find themselves in trouble.

Here are some of the typical difficulties the church encounters:

• **The volunteers can't keep up with the schedule.** Why? Because of the nature of the word *volunteer*. They may be doing the work after hours from their "real" jobs. They may be retired but have other responsibilities. They may be parents and have Little League or rehearsals or other activities that require their time. And yet you have hired contractors that are scheduling *their* work around your volunteers. The contractors are waiting for the painting, the insulation, or the drywall to be finished. Once a contractor pulls off your job to someone else's project, it's difficult to get him back.

• **The ability of the volunteer isn't what you expected, and the quality of the project suffers.** It's a sad day when you walk in and see that the rooms that were just painted by your volunteers have to be repainted. And, worse yet, you have to tell the volunteers, "Your work isn't good enough. Go home." But really, it's not their fault—it's yours.

• **The volunteers feel used by the end of the project.** They have great hearts and just want to help, but now they feel pushed. It's not very fun anymore. It's not very gratifying to give when the giving is expected. Even so, you have to push them because they aren't moving quickly enough for your contractor.

Here are some suggestions for handling volunteers in this situation:

• **Utilize their gifts and availability on smaller projects** that don't require coordination with a contractor or are not time-sensitive.

• When you have skilled and reputable contractors in the church who want to donate services to the church, **encourage them to submit their discounted bids to the general contractor.** Take yourself out of the loop. Make the general contractor responsible for quality and schedule. The only workers or suppliers from the congregation you should use are those you would select even if they were not part of the church. And they should be held to the same standard as every other worker.

• **Check references.** Always. Always. Always. Even if you've been attending church with these people for twenty years, you need to check their professional references.

Working with volunteers on your project doesn't have to be a problem. Implement some of these suggestions, and you'll create a win for the volunteers as well as for the project.

—Tim

33 Sack the No-Huddle Offense

Once you've pulled your team together, you need to sack the no-huddle offense. You need to create times for your teams to meet regularly. These gatherings will offer opportunities for you to not only share vision and define strategies for accomplishing your action plan, but also care for the members of your team. For many people, a ministry team will be the only connection they have within your church. They won't be in a discipleship relationship. They won't be in a small group or Sunday school class,

> Create times for your teams to meet regularly.

but they will be a part of a ministry team. Don't miss this chance to find out what's happening in their lives, including the steps they may or may not be taking in their faith journeys. This could very well be the only chance they have to be encouraged to pursue spiritual maturity.

At Granger, some of our ministry teams meet weekly. Some meet every four to six weeks. Our staff teams try to model these gatherings for the lay leaders. Our Senior Management Team (SMT) meets once a week. The SMT meets with the associate staff leaders, our director-level leaders, once a month. We come together for all-staff gatherings every month as well. Within departments, team gatherings take place on a regular basis.

The format of these meetings is different in each setting. For example, when I gather with the other pastors on the SMT, our agenda includes these types of items:

• **Updates.** What's happening in your life? How can we pray for you? What's happening in your ministry area that will affect the rest of us? What are your dreams for the future?

• **Evaluation.** How are we doing as a church? Are we healthy in all five biblical purposes? Are we continuing to see balanced growth throughout the ministry? Are we on track with our mission, vision, and values?

- **Strategy.** What are the ministry priorities? How can we help people take their next spiritual steps to become fully devoted followers of Christ?
- **Planning.** What's our action plan? What will it take to accomplish the three or four specific projects, events, or programs we're going to focus on in the next six months?
- **Decisions.** Who's responsible? What investments are needed? When will we do it? How will we monitor progress?
- **Fun.** What can we do away from the office just to reconnect on a personal level, let loose, and get refreshed for the next run of ministry?

As the size of the gatherings grows, the agenda changes. Larger gatherings include more vision casting, training, and fun stuff to build teamwork. Planning and decision making can't take place in these settings.

> It takes discipline to gather regularly because there's never a good time to pull away from *doing* ministry to *talk* about ministry.

It takes discipline to gather regularly because there's never a good time to pull away from *doing* ministry to *talk* about ministry. The fact is, however, these team gatherings will help focus your efforts and allow your ministry to bear more fruit. Additionally, you'll have the chance to bring encouragement and accountability to others on your team. Don't forget to huddle up.

—Tony

34

Give Your Staff Cool Gifts

Last year we bought Dottie a portable crib to help her care for her new grandchild. We bought Mark a pair of cool binoculars he's always wanted. We gave Karen a gift certificate to her favorite online store. Rob was surprised when we bought him the *Twilight Zone* DVDs.

We decided a long time ago that we wanted our staff to "feel" the love of the church all year long. When they are tired or frustrated or out of energy, we want them to know they are valued. Their lives matter. So we surprise them with unexpected gifts.

This is *not* a bonus. It is *not* a result of their job performance. It is because of their lives, and it is because of our love.

You might say, "They need the money in their paychecks. I'd rather just increase their pay." However, once you establish their paycheck, it becomes an expectation. When you say, "We are going to pay you $30,000 next year," they expect that paycheck. They budget for their living expenses based on what you said you would pay. Although it is a blessing and a provision of God, it still becomes an expectation. They don't get all excited and feel your love every time they receive a paycheck. It becomes routine. It is expected.

If your budget for a position is $30,000, you can tell the person you'll pay $29,000 so you can hold back $1,000 to bless him or her throughout the year with gifts. Put it in your budget, but keep it a surprise. Then you can surprise the person with a gift certificate in April, free rounds of golf in July, and an overnight package with his or her spouse in October.

Here are more tips that may help:

• **Consult your tax adviser or accountant** to make sure you're reporting these gifts as income. As such, they are taxable to the employee.

• **Try to avoid giving the gifts at Christmastime.** They will be less expected and more appreciated when received throughout the year.

• **Deliver the gifts personally** so you can communicate how much the recipients are loved by you and the church.

> Communicate this message openly: "We take care of our staff!"

• **Build this into your budget.** Don't try to convince a committee or board every year of the need. Convince them once, put it in the budget, and make it a part of the culture of your church. Communicate this message openly: "We take care of our staff!"

Do this, and you will be communicating all year long how valuable your staff is. It doesn't have to cost any more money than you are already budgeting. Just hold back a few hundred dollars to shower the staff with unexpected gifts throughout the year.

—Tim

35 Your Web Site Today Shouldn't Be Seen Tomorrow

People need a reason to return to your Web site. They'll come back either because they know they'll find the latest information or because they have an opportunity for interaction there. If they return to your site and find the same general church information that you had on the site last week, they won't come back. The objective is to create a Web site that allows people to interact with your ministry and with one another.

As you're developing your site, remember your three target audiences:

• **People checking out your church.** There are people who just want to know the basics about your church. They're trying to figure out what to expect if they visit. They want to know about the services, what to wear, what will happen with their kids, and how long they'll have to stay. They'll need the location, times, and a way to contact you for more details. Share a little bit about "who you are" in simple, easy-to-understand words.

• **People trying to connect to your church.** These are people who have already started attending your church and are now wanting to connect in membership, relationships, or ministry. They want to know where to go next. For this group, information about classes, groups, and your various ministry areas will be most helpful.

• **People who are committed to your church.** This group is looking for the latest information about what's happening in your ministry. They're looking for news and the schedule of events. They want additional resources that will supplement their weekend service experience, including devotionals, discussion guides, and forums for additional interaction.

Here are a handful of our favorite church Web sites that you can visit to see how they're communicating with these target audiences:

• Fellowship Church—www.fellowshipchurch.com

- Point of Grace—www.pointofgrace.org
- Saddleback Church—www.saddleback.com
- Mosaic—www.mosaic.org
- Westwinds Community Church—www.westwinds.org
- Eagle Brook Church—www.eaglebrookchurch.com
- Granger Community Church—www.gccwired.com

As you're visiting these sites, take note of these features: You can get to the critical information with very few mouse clicks, the navigation systems are easy to use, the sites are laid out consistently from page to page, the focus is on people rather than buildings, and the information is current.

When designing Web sites, remember that flashy isn't necessarily better.

When designing Web sites, remember that flashy isn't necessarily better. Typically, simple Web sites with a few quality graphics are better than sites that are loaded with lots of functions working simultaneously. It's kind of the equivalent of creating "white space" in print layout. Simplicity helps draw attention to the critical information your target audience is seeking. It also keeps your site fast, which should always be a primary focus. It's also important to consider maintenance as you're developing your site. Someone has to be in charge of the content to make sure your Web site has the current news before anyone else does. Your Web site should be the first place people go to find out who you are and what you're doing.

Keep your Web site fresh. Make sure it has the latest information. If visitors see the same thing on your Web site today that they saw yesterday, they probably won't visit again tomorrow.

—Tony

36 Giving Is Personal—Not Private

I've heard many pastors say with pride, "I don't know the giving records of anyone in our church. I want to be able to treat and speak to people equally without giving favor to some because of the amount of money they give."

This sounds great and preaches well. It gives people in the congregation a sense of awe at the pastor's purity of heart. People feel good that the pastor is not motivated by money and won't get caught up with catering to those who use their money to control. However, I really question whether it is wise.

Here are questions I would ask those pastors:

• Do you treat those who give of their time and abilities in the same way? Do you say that you don't want to cater to those who volunteer twenty hours a week more than to those who don't volunteer at all?

• Do you value the spiritual gift of giving less than other spiritual gifts? Should those who have given of their teaching or administration or serving gifts get more attention from you than those who have exercised their gift of giving?

• Do you care if you have a lay leader or staff member who is robbing God of the tithe? Would it bother you if you knew? Giving is one of the only tangible pictures God has given us that directly reflect a person's heart condition. How can you help individuals take spiritual steps if you leave out this reflection of their hearts?

> Giving is one of the only tangible pictures God has given us that directly reflect a person's heart condition.

Although many churches enthusiastically embrace an I-don't-know-what-you-give policy, I really think they miss out on key opportunities to lead. Consider these factors:

• There really are people with the spiritual gift of giving. Just as you would affirm musicians or nursery workers because they give their time and abilities, you should recognize those who give their finances. This might include an occasional handwritten thank-you note or planning one-on-one times to learn more about them and their families.

• You need a policy in place that lets you know when key leaders aren't tithing. If they aren't tithing, then the Bible says there is a heart problem. Trouble may be brewing. It could be personal financial problems, in which case you can help them through a tough time. It could be a heart problem, and you may have an opportunity to help them heal before it's too late. (Often, pastors don't find out about problems until these people leave the church. If the pastors had looked at the giving records, they would have seen it coming and could have provided help and healing.)

• If you are the senior pastor, there may be people in your church whom only you can reach. Because of their financial or business success, some individuals are accustomed to dealing with the "top person" in any organization. Because of your position, you may be the one most likely to help them take spiritual steps. Knowing their giving records will help you identify them.

Teach your people that giving is very personal, but it is not private. Tell them that you will treat their giving records with confidentiality, but don't make promises about who will or won't see the data. Put systems in place that will protect you and the church from being controlled by a wealthy member, but also put in place systems that will allow you to use giving as one measurement of a person's heart condition.

—Tim

37 It's Easier to Tame the Lions Than Prod the Turtles

"Lazy people are a pain to their employer. They are like smoke in the eyes or vinegar that sets the teeth on edge" (Proverbs 10:26, NLT).

I recently read an Associated Press article about sick leave usage in Sweden. It indicated that government-paid sick leave benefits are so good there that the number of people taking advantage of the benefit has doubled in the last five years. The program now accounts for 16 percent of the national budget. As a result, a recent survey indicated 60 percent of Swedes believe it's acceptable to call in sick even if they aren't ill.

Bad systems can promote poor work habits. In addition to that, we have to realize that people are different. Some people just put in their time. They do the bare minimum. When the clock strikes five, they're out the door. They are frequently absent. When you delegate a task, you know you'll have to follow up or it won't get done.

On the other hand, other people will always go the extra mile. They show up early, work hard all day, and put in extra hours when necessary. Many days, you almost have to force them to call it quits. These people are focused and driven. They want to get the job done and make sure it's done right.

Of course, a good work ethic can also lead to problems. People can become so focused on doing ministry that they lose balance in their relationships with families, friends, and Jesus. My experience, however, is that it's easier to help people regain balance than it is to teach a good work ethic.

With that in mind, try to surround yourself with people who tend toward imbalance in their work habits. Find the recovering workaholics, and then develop a culture that encourages and emphasizes balance and health.

—Tony

38 Build Your Church Before You Build Your Church

Rick Warren, pastor of Saddleback Church, says that most churches build "too soon and too small." It's understandable. Bricks and mortar contribute to a church's status and sense of accomplishment and give new churches a sense of legitimacy. We have something to point to when we're telling friends about our church. Those of us who have rented space for church services have heard people say, "Tell me when you are in your own building, and I might visit then."

But the church *building* isn't the church, is it? The church is a living organism. It is the people. It is those who have given their lives to Christ and have gathered locally to make a difference in their communities. There are churches all over the world that have no buildings or facilities and yet are living, thriving local churches!

> There are churches all over the world that have no buildings or facilities and yet are living, thriving local churches!

Putting up a building before the church is ready could cause troubles down the road. Do the following before you consider breaking ground:

- Define your mission, vision, and values.
- Build broad ownership of these defined values through your entire core of believers.
- Make sure that your leadership team is strong and growing.
- Develop a culture of volunteerism.
- Develop an infrastructure of leaders and systems that can handle the demands of a facility.
- Take the spiritual temperature of your church, and make sure that the people are continuing to take spiritual steps.

There are some great advantages to renting space for your services. It teaches your people flexibility and encourages a pioneering spirit. It allows for cheap growth. If you find a space large enough, you can continue to grow for months or years without the costly maintenance and operations of a building. It gives you a chance to teach your people that "building a church" isn't about construction or architecture. It lets you focus on the importance of people and not on bricks and mortar.

If you feel a growing pressure within you to build a facility, be sure to check your motives. Is it for image? Is it for personal reputation? Is it to prove that something significant is going on at your church? Is it to give you something to brag about at gatherings of area pastors?

Make sure that having a facility will serve the purposes of God in your community. Make sure that it will facilitate reaching more and more people for Christ. Remember, the church is a living organism made up of the people Christ died for. A building is only beneficial if the people are thriving.

—Tim

34 Deliver the Game Plan

Granger Community Church is located in the shadow of the Golden Dome. The Notre Dame campus is less than ten minutes from the church. And if you associate only one thing with Notre Dame, it's probably football.

Unfortunately, recent years haven't been so kind to Irish football fans. In 2001, the team finally hit bottom, at least by Notre Dame standards, by finishing with only five wins and no bowl-game invitations. They fired their coach. Then they tried to hire another only to learn he had misrepresented his credentials on his résumé. The program was in a tailspin.

That's when the university finally turned to Tyrone Willingham. Willingham, who had spent the previous seven years coaching at Stanford, immediately came in and put his mark on the football program. In his very first press conference on New Year's Day 2002, he began to cast his vision for the team's return to glory:

"Everything that we do is about winning....we're about winning on the field, yes. Winning in the classroom, yes. But also winning in terms of young men's social and spiritual development."

As I write, the football team has just finished upsetting Florida State to start the 2002 season with eight straight wins—this with essentially the same players that failed to make a bowl game last year. What's made the difference? There are many, but I believe one of the keys is that the team has recaptured its vision. It expects to win, both on the field and in life.

So where is your ministry going? Is your vision for developing fully devoted followers of Christ as clearly defined as Coach Willingham's vision for developing champions on and off the football field? It should be. Your team is ready to take the field and is waiting for you to share the game plan. It's time for you to define God's calling for your ministry and communicate that vision often. Your team is counting on you.

—Tony

40 When You Discover Sin in the Leadership, Don't Cover It Up

"I can hardly believe the report about the sexual immorality going on among you, something so evil that even the pagans don't do it...Why aren't you mourning in sorrow and shame? And why haven't you removed this man from your fellowship?" (1 Corinthians 5:1a, 2b, NLT).

It was May 2002. The daily headlines around the United States were about the sex scandals and coverups in the Catholic Church. And on a Thursday night at Granger we were only two hours away from the start of the single biggest annual musical event at our church. That's when we got the report: One of our key pastors was involved in deep immorality. Within twenty-four hours we learned that it was not a one-time incident, but rather a pattern of wrong choices and sinful actions over the previous two years.

We had several options available to us.

• We could ignore it.

• We could handle it quietly. We could help our fallen pastor but not take any action that would alarm the church.

• We could dismiss the pastor but hide the reason. No one had to know. The official explanation could be "He is dealing with some personal issues in his life and will be stepping out of ministry."

• We could care enough to be completely honest. We could leave no room for gossip and lift high the banner for integrity in the church by covering *nothing* up.

After seeking counsel from several pastors who had faced these types of issues and after much prayer and discussion, we chose the last option. It was Mother's Day, and we had just mailed thirty thousand invitations to the community to attend the launch of a new series. However, we cancelled the plans for the weekend and took the entire service to address the issue of sin in leadership. We were completely honest about the sin, when we found out about it, the steps we were taking to help with restoration, how we were caring for the family of our fallen friend, how the church should respond, and our expectation of integrity in leadership. We communicated with love and compassion but called for holiness and righteous living.

This is the guiding principle: Don't cover up sin in leadership. The coverup will cause more harm than the sin.

Here are some guidelines to help you:

• **The sphere of the individual's influence dictates the scope of the confession.** If it is a small-group leader, then don't go to the whole church. Instead, go to the small group and perhaps other small-group leaders. If it is a children's ministry leader, then handle it in the children's ministry. If it is a pastor or leader who has influence over the whole church, then you must handle it openly and honestly with the entire church. Even seekers will respect your action if you tell the truth delicately.

• **If it is a sin that could expose the church to legal action, be sure to get legal counsel.** For example, if you find out about a child molestation, handle it quickly and honestly, but do so in consultation with a Christian attorney.

• **Get counsel.** Talk to church leaders who have gone through this. Don't go down this road alone. Get guidance from those who have already traveled this path.

Now, several months after our crisis, we do not know of one member who left the church because of how we handled the situation. Instead, our attendance has grown by over seven hundred, and the church today is stronger and healthier than it has ever been. In today's culture, no one is surprised when someone messes up. People are watching, though, to see if the church handles these situations differently than politicians or corporations. Follow our advice, and don't cover up sin.

—Tim

41 Keep Budgeting Simple

Here's a common thread I've found in all churches: Only the finance people like the budget process. For everyone else, it's a necessary evil that must be addressed once a year, like it or not. Because of that, you need to keep your budget process as simple as possible. Here are the key ingredients to a simple process.

Start with a schedule. Determine when the board must make the final decision, then work backward. Try to keep the process as short as possible while leaving room for prayer and decision making. Your primary focus is ministry. You don't need people involved in perpetual budget mode. Eight weeks should be enough.

Assign responsibility. Delegate the development of the budget to each of your ministry leaders. The same person who submits the budget proposal will also be responsible for approving all expenditures and making sure the ministry area stays within the approved budget.

Define your action plan. Don't begin with numbers. Begin with action plans. Determine what the hot projects will be for the next twelve months. Decide what you want each ministry area to accomplish, and then figure out how much it will cost. This process keeps the focus on the future. It makes ministry outcomes the top priority rather than the continuation of last year's programs, which may or may not still be effective.

Create simple forms. Collect only as much detail as you'll need to adequately manage and monitor budget performance. Develop easy-to-use forms to collect the details for each account, and then capture the details in a summary worksheet. Use the same forms throughout the ministry. Automate them whenever possible. If your computers are connected to a computer network, your office management software can easily create forms that can be published to the file server for all leaders to easily access. Your budget point person needs to be familiar with technology to streamline the process as much as possible.

Make as few decisions as possible. Collect the proposals. Decide how you're going to allocate the resources, including money and staff. And give the final decision for meeting budget targets back to the various ministry leaders. Once the budget is balanced, provide it to the board for final approval along with the ministry action plan for the coming year. Tie the dollars to anticipated outcomes.

Don't begin with numbers. Begin with action plans.

Remember, the budget is only a plan. It does not define reality. With that in mind, the ministry programs should be responsible only for the bottom line. It's a fruitless exercise in micromanagement to make leaders accountable for every line item. Let them know it's OK to go over budget on specific line items as long as they don't exceed the bottom line at the end of the year. Additionally, the budget should include flexibility for developing new ideas and addressing emergency situations. Don't let ministries pad each line item. Instead, plan general contingency accounts to address the unexpected.

Budgeting offers a great opportunity to strategically plan for the future. Focus on developing dreams rather than grinding through the details. In the end you'll have a better plan, and the process will be less overwhelming for your ministry leaders.

—Tony

42 Make "Hellos" Long and "Goodbyes" Quick

You can't interview too much or ask too many questions when you are bringing on a key staff person. You should interview many times, ask hard questions, contact references, ask references for more references, and call them, too. Stretch out the "hello" as long as necessary for you to be 100 percent comfortable with your decision.

The "goodbye," however, is an entirely different deal. Even in the best of situations, it's very tough to end a staff relationship. We've developed friendships and experienced life together. We never imagined that we wouldn't be doing ministry together for years and years. But, for some reason, God has taken our paths in two separate directions. It is always a temptation to draw out the goodbye process. We want to throw parties and ask the people who are leaving to stay until we've replaced them. We don't want them to leave, so we prolong their departure.

There are other times, however, when we really do want them to leave quickly, but we don't want to appear uncaring or heartless. We don't want to be perceived as having "kicked them out" of their jobs and their offices. So, to save face, we give them a month...or three months...or as long as it takes.

This all stems from great intentions. However, our experience has indicated that it is best to make the departure time *very* fast. In most situations, for pastoral or key staff positions, we would recommend no more than two weeks.

There are two very important reasons for this:

1. People who are departing become a magnet for every unhappy person in your church. Whether they are leaving on good or bad terms, those who have complaints will assume they are leaving for the complainers' own reasons. So they will begin to unload on departing staff members. They will look for a comrade to side with. They will gossip with others, pretending they have "inside information" from the former staff member.

2. Departing staff members can no longer dream about the future

of your ministry. They become dead weight within hours of the announcement. There will be no additional conversations about new ways to reach more people for Christ or creative ways to do the Christmas series. They're no longer interested in plans for next year's men's retreat. No...their dreams are, understandably, somewhere else.

So pay them for as long as you'd like. Extend their benefits, pay their health insurance, and mail them their paychecks. When it comes to their offices and official staff roles, however, set their final date within two weeks of their notice.

—Tim

43 Tell Stories

It had become fairly routine. I would stand up at the beginning of the midweek service, targeted for followers of Christ, and make the announcements. Oh, we don't call them announcements. We call that portion of the service "family time" or "strategic concerns." But, in reality, it's announcements.

Typically during this time people are arriving, getting settled, and taking off coats. After three or four minutes, they are finally beginning to focus and become aware that someone on the stage is talking.

On this particular night several years ago, I decided to start with a story. I talked about how Jesus became real to me when I attended camp as a young boy. The story might have lasted sixty to ninety seconds. Then I transitioned into an announcement about scholarships that were needed for our junior high camp.

I was utterly amazed. Not fifteen seconds into the story, the auditorium was silent. All six hundred pairs of eyes were looking at me. People were engaged in the story. They were listening as though sitting on the edge of their seats. They would smile or laugh or groan at appropriate times in the story. I had them.

That experience marked me, and I learned a valuable lesson. Stories draw people in. Stories are remembered. Stories help us focus. I have never stood up since then to make an announcement without telling a story. Sometimes it lasts only twenty seconds, but I always tell a story or give an illustration.

Here are some things to consider when it comes to storytelling:

- Jesus' primary style of communication was through stories.
- Tell stories about the changed lives of people in your congregation.
- Use stories along with statistics or business reports.
- Use stories when you are thanking

> I have never stood up since then to make an announcement without telling a story.

people for giving. They need to know the impact of their investments.

• A good rule of thumb for preaching is to divide the length of your sermon by five, then make sure you have that many stories. For example, in a thirty-minute message, you'll have six stories. People will stay engaged!

• Make sure you use stories of your personal mistakes, not just your successes. People want to know that you are human.

By the way, did you notice that I started this chapter with a story about telling a story to emphasize the power of telling stories? Now you can tell a story about a guy who told a story about the time he had told a story...

You get the point.

—Tim

44 Watch These Three Lids

There are three "lids" that will prevent a growing church from sustaining its growth. It doesn't matter how good your weekend services or your adult discipleship programs are. It doesn't matter how great your youth ministry is or how many attend your annual Christmas production. If you aren't able to address these three lids on a continual basis, your church will eventually stop growing.

Lid 1: Parking. If it's difficult for newcomers to go to your church, they won't go. If they have a bad experience getting into your building or getting out of the parking lot, they won't return. Lifelong church attendees may not care if they have to park in the gravel and walk three blocks, but if you are going to reach new people, you will need to make their experience pleasant.

Lid 2: Children. If you have a space problem, either real or perceived, then your growth will be limited until the problem is addressed. Parents care about their children and therefore want them in a safe, secure environment. They want them to have personal attention. They want them to succeed and to thrive. If it looks like a child is entering a room that is too small, understaffed, or unsafe, then the parents of that child will not return. As a result, your growth will be hindered.

Lid 3: Seats. We've all heard the "80 percent rule." Church experts have said for decades, "When your auditorium reaches 80 percent full, you are at capacity." Your growth will begin to level off when your space is 80 percent full. For years, I tried to disprove this theory. I wanted our church to be the exception to the rule. But over time, I found it to be true of Granger as well. At 80 percent capacity in our auditorium, a married couple or a family of three will not be able to sit together. It's not likely that their experience will be enjoyable, and they probably won't return.

What are the next three or four lids at your church? How will you address them? Many times, when you "lift" one lid by adding parking or seats or classrooms, you will face the next lid very quickly. Do you have a "lid watcher"? Every growing church should have someone who is constantly watching these three lids and looking into the future.

—Tim

Most Designated Gifts Should Be Turned Down

In some instances, designated giving can be beneficial. For example, it can help people learn the value of sacrificial giving. Sometimes people will make their first real contributions to your church if they can match their contributions with one of their passions. On the other hand, designated giving can lead to problems. Namely, you run the risk that someone will begin to control the ministry by attaching restrictions to how the money can be used. Or people may expect that they have decision-making input because of the size of their financial support to a particular program or project. Additionally, a menu approach of giving to specific ministries in the church may lead to cash-flow problems. For example, although people may feel good about giving to a new youth program, that youth program won't be effective if the church can't pay the electric bill.

Teach people that their financial gifts will benefit the entire church, not just their favorite ministries.

With that in mind, you need to establish guidelines to encourage healthy, biblical stewardship while at the same time promoting a unified budget—one that supports all programming and operations expenses. You need to teach people that their financial gifts will benefit the entire church, not just their favorite ministries. And that places the burden on the senior pastor to effectively communicate the vision for the church. Once that happens, people will be more inclined to give to the overall vision rather than to their pet project.

One way you can guide designated giving and prevent it from getting out of hand is to preapprove appropriate areas for designated gifts. We have only two areas in which we accept gifts that are not part of the general offering. One designated giving option is for missions. Each month, we specify a different agency, trip, or benevolence fund that will benefit from gifts marked "missions." This offers an opportunity for people to give directly to others in need. The other area of designated gifts is for stewardship campaigns. These are established to allow people to help us expand our ministry campus.

Beyond preapproved giving, you should ask this critical question anytime someone offers a gift for a specific program or project: "Will this gift help us fulfill the vision by addressing a current ministry priority?" If the answer is yes, establish a process for receiving and tracking the expenditure of that money. Make sure the money is used as it was intended. If the answer is no, do your best to explain to the donor why you can't accept the gift, and take the opportunity to cast vision for the overall ministry of the church.

Be proactive about communicating vision and teaching the tithe. Don't let designated gifts drive the ministry priorities of your church.

—Tony

46 The Journey Is as Important as the Destination

cause, *n.* 1. our mission as a church.

community, *n.* 1. our life together as we accomplish the cause.

Consider these definitions. Church leaders place varying levels of importance on cause and community. Which of the following best represents your belief?

1. Community is significantly more important than cause.
2. Community is slightly more important than cause.
3. Cause and community are of equal importance.
4. Cause is slightly more important than community.
5. Cause is significantly more important than community.

Most pastors I meet will initially circle statement 5. It is how we are taught. There is a lost world going to hell, and we are charged as Christians and as pastors with telling the world about Jesus. The cause is huge. In fact, I believe there is no greater cause.

But many times, we forget that in order to *build* a church, we must *be* the church. We must love one another. We must encourage one another. We must work through hard times together. We must celebrate success and mourn failure together. We have to pray together and cry together and love together and learn together. If we are to build a church that represents Jesus' heart to the world, we must model that!

In the past few months, I personally heard a pastor say to his staff members, "Just get the damn job done." Another said, "I will not be your friend; I will be your boss."

Statements like these, in my opinion, stem from past hurt. They are defensive words used in an effort to protect the speaker from more pain. But so much is lost. The potential joy of close, intimate relationships with other Christians is forfeited. Instead, it is a business relationship. And the church we are trying to lead does not get to see what the church should look like.

It's definitely harder to emphasize community. It's messy. It has the potential for hurt, pain, and even bitterness. It always requires honest communication, and sometimes these conversations are difficult. It may mean entering conversations about feelings and perception when you'd rather talk about methods and job performance. But if we can create a culture valuing integrity in meaningful relationships, then we will have something tangible that reflects God's intention for his church.

Mark Beeson has taught this many times, and my wife and I have adopted it as a parenting principle. When we load up the car for a long trip, we give a speech that goes something like this: "Here we go, kids! The fun begins today. The adventure starts right now. Don't wait until we get there to have fun. It won't get any better than this. Let's take our fun with us, starting this very minute!" Our kids are learning to value the journey.

Is the journey truly as important as the destination? I don't know. I do, however, believe that in many ways, the journey is the destination. It is about *where* we are going—but it is also about how we live along the way.

—Tim

47 Focus on Hot Projects

When the church tries to do everything, it often ends up doing nothing. When the church focuses on the right thing and does it well, it transforms lives. The question is, "What are you going to do in the next six to twelve months?" What are the projects, events, or ministry initiatives that are going to be the focus of your prayers, your time, and your resources? What's next on your agenda?

> When the church focuses on the right thing and does it well, it transforms lives.

You need hot projects. These are the steppingstones to your preferred future. They move your church beyond the daily grind of "doing church" and help you move toward fulfilling your vision. In smaller churches it may be only one project. In the largest of churches, it's probably not more than three to five at any one time. Examples include a specific community outreach event, adding a new weekend service, and constructing the next phase of your building. Not everyone in the congregation may be involved in the projects, but everyone should know about them and be praying for God to provide wisdom, resources, and results.

Our church's current hot projects include implementing a new Web strategy, launching a new class to help people define their life purpose, and giving one hundred thousand pounds of food to the community. Another church I recently visited will be tackling two hot projects in the next twelve months. One is transitioning from a committee-led to a staff-led structure. The other is implementing a new adult-ministry plan that creates large group gatherings and helps move people into small-group experiences. That's it. They'll continue to hold services. The youth will still meet. They may still have a wedding or two, but their primary focus will be those two projects. They won't try to tack on anything else.

For these initiatives to be successful, you need to identify several key components.

• **Vision.** Everyone should know up front how this ministry focus fits the vision and strategy of the church. You need to communicate. It's a time to cast vision.

• **Project champion.** You also need to identify a project champion, someone who is ultimately responsible for the success of the initiative.

> Without hot projects, a church's normal tendency is to fall into a routine.

• **Deadline.** Every project needs a time frame for completion.

• **Resources.** You also need to deploy resources such as staff support, volunteers, money, equipment, and space.

• **Measures.** You need to establish measurable targets to determine outcomes and success.

Without these hot projects, a church's normal tendency is to fall into a routine. Incremental changes and improvements may occur, but generally life goes on today just as it did yesterday. There's nothing wrong with incremental change. There's a place for efficiency. But time is short, and there's a world of people who need to know Jesus. So how are you going to spend your time today? If you don't know, it may be time to identify your hot projects.

—Tony

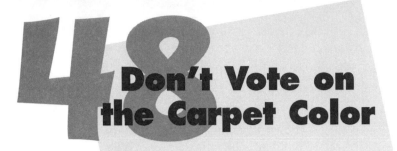

Don't Vote on the Carpet Color

Here are some truths about people:

• They have opinions.

• If you ask their opinion, they'll tell you.

• People tend to group with others who share their opinions.

• If you ask their opinion, and then choose differently, many times they'll feel devalued or hurt. Or they'll think you are stupid.

Does that mean we should never ask for opinions or advice? Absolutely not. But it's best to save the question for important and relevant issues.

When I was much younger, I worked for Life Action Ministries. I traveled the country ten months each year ministering in churches. In my nine years with Life Action, I visited more than one thousand churches. I heard lots of stories about church splits and business meetings that went awry. I was at one church, for example, whose congregants voted on the color of the carpet and then split because they couldn't agree. I visited another congregation that voted on the size of the kitchen and then split because, you guessed it, they couldn't agree. I heard about churches that voted on playgrounds and parking lots and wedding chapels and hallways. And I heard about the fights that broke out and the feelings that were hurt as a result. Years later, people were still talking about the arguments.

Here is my advice: Don't bring nonessential issues to the congregation, board, or committee for a vote. Find trustworthy and capable people, and let them make the decisions. Don't send meaningless decisions about colors, fabric selections, or the carpet texture to a committee for approval. Furthermore, you shouldn't try to convince yourself that such decisions are crucial to your mission or purpose as a church. If you can't find capable people whom you trust to make those decisions, then you may have a leadership problem in the church. Keep your congregation focused on its mission and purpose, and don't allow it to be bogged down with the nonessentials.

—Tim

49 Systems Should Make Life Easier

Several years ago, when I was still working in local government, the fire department was working on its standard operating procedures. That was a good thing, because procedures are helpful during emergency situations. After the fire alarm sounds, there shouldn't be any question or argument about equipment, responsibilities, and tactics. Those are the decisions that firefighters need to make in advance. I had to laugh one day, though, because the guys working on the project came to me with what they thought was a positive addition to their procedures manual. They had created a standard operating procedure for creating standard operating procedures—essentially a policy for making policy. That's when you know life is more complicated than it needs to be.

The best systems and procedures help people become more effective and efficient in their ministry roles. If routine can bring order to chaos, that's helpful. If, on the other hand, it just creates another hoop for people to jump through, you're moving in the wrong direction.

To be honest, church administrators are usually notorious for overreacting to every situation and trying to create policy to avert future problems. Everything in life doesn't need to be black and white. Sometimes gray is appropriate because some issues are really better handled on a case-by-case basis. Lots of policies create lots of bureaucracy and little ministry fruit.

> Church administrators are notorious for overreacting to every situation and trying to create policy to avert future problems.

Every time you create a new policy, you should ask two fundamental questions: (1) Do we actually need this policy? and (2) does it make life easier for our team? Systems should make life easier—not harder. If you answer yes to both of these questions, you're moving in the right direction and eliminating the barriers that would otherwise stop growth in your church.

Systems are helpful in several areas of ministry. Some examples are membership, connecting people with ministry and others, purchasing, hiring, and processing contributions. You shouldn't have to re-create the process every time someone wants to join your church, for example. There should already be a system in place.

The challenge for leaders is to routinely evaluate the decisions they are making and determine whether a system could move that responsibility to others in the ministry. Obviously, there are some decisions the senior leadership team should never give away; however, good systems will free up your staff leaders and the church board to focus on the future and the big-picture issues.

—Tony

50 Put "Professional Cheerleader" on Your Business Card

Pastors and church leaders are best known for their roles as preacher, teacher, leader, or prayer warrior. Sometimes, however, they are talked about in ways that aren't as appealing. Here are some examples:

"He is such a perfectionist. No one can live up to his standards."

"It's impossible to make him happy."

"When she teaches, she always seems mad and judgmental."

"She always seems upset at someone."

"He is a great preacher, but I'd hate to work for him."

Why is it so rare that a pastor is described as an encourager, trainer, or mentor? Why are some church members afraid to serve or use their gifts? What would happen if pastors took on "cheerleader" as their primary role? What if they decided their chief responsibility was to encourage and affirm their people? How radical a change would that be for most people?

Mark Beeson started Granger Community Church in 1986 as a cheerleader, and he hasn't dropped that role since those early days. His life is characterized by encouragement. Standing behind the pulpit or walking in the hallway, he is a cheerleader.

Here is a sample of a normal Sunday morning for Mark:

- Parks his car and thanks Marcia, the parking lot shuttle driver, for giving up her Sunday morning to help people in the parking lot.

- Walks up the front walk and tells Bob and Jan, two of the greeters, how great they are.

- Passes Luann, a nursery worker, and lets her know what a difference she'll make in the lives of little ones today.

- Stops and talks to Craig, a saxophone player, and tells him he's making a difference. "Keep up the good work," he says.

- Sees Michelle, who sang a solo last week, and tells her what a great impact the solo had.

- Sits in the front row next to Verne, who helps with stage props, and thanks him for giving up his weekend to sit through every service.

- Walks onto the stage after a drama and leads the crowd in thanking the actors for preparing the way for the message.

- Talks for thirty minutes, encouraging everyone to take their next step. Makes people feel loved—not judged.

- After the service, encourages several more people on his way to his office. Sits down and writes three postcards thanking individuals for their participation in this weekend's mission.

This is a "professional cheerleader" who is pastoring and leading a church. There is something to be learned from his example. Remember, the preaching, teaching, and leading roles of a pastor are important, but the role of cheerleader is also vital to your ministry.

—Tim

51 It's Easier to Hire Than to Fire

This is a true story. Several years ago we received a call from an executive pastor at a large church. He was calling to let us know his church was considering hiring one of our guys for a pastoral role. He wanted to find out about strengths and weaknesses and make sure he was pursuing the right person for the role. It's a pretty smart thing to do. Reference checks are a key component to any selection process. The only problem in this case was that our guy had already been offered the job and had accepted. He was already packing for the move, but his new executive pastor didn't know he had joined the team. Oops.

Fortunately, that church has continued to grow and all is good, but this example points to the need for establishing a system for adding staff. This is particularly true as your church grows. Here are the basic steps that we follow at Granger:

• **Position request.** When a ministry team wants to fill a staff vacancy, the supervisor submits a request in writing to the executive pastor, outlining the proposed position, hours of work, and recommended wage level. The executive pastor must approve the position before advertising and recruiting may begin.

• **Position classification and wage level.** The senior pastor and executive pastor determine all position classifications and wage levels. This includes determining whether the position will be included with the senior management team, associate staff, or support staff.

• **Interviews and selection.** The supervisor is responsible for recruiting, interviewing, administering appropriate skill tests, and checking references. We typically conduct interviews as a team, which includes the supervisor and one or more others to provide additional feedback. We provide sample interview questions, evaluation forms, and reference-check forms for the supervisors as needed. The supervisor selects the top candidate and submits a written request to the executive pastor for final approval.

• **Employee orientation.** After receiving approval from the executive pastor, we distribute an employee-orientation checklist which outlines, among other things, a review of roles and expectations as well as training assignments for building security, computers, and telephones. Additionally, the checklist details the forms that each new employee must complete on or before the first day of employment.

Most of these guidelines should also apply as you're filling key volunteer leadership positions. Define the role, including responsibilities and expectations. Conduct an interview to determine whether the candidate's gifts, experiences, personality, and passion are a good fit with the position. Check references to confirm or challenge what you learned in the interview. Provide an orientation session to equip and empower your new leader. These steps will not only ensure that you find the right people to fill your volunteer roles; they will also communicate the value of the position even though there will be no monetary compensation.

Launch your recruitment process with a predetermined plan. It's always a lot easier to hire the right person than it is to fire the wrong person.

—Tony

52 Take Me to Your Leader

At Granger, the members of our Senior Management Team provide not only organizational leadership to the ministry, but also spiritual leadership, serving as the elders of the church. With that in mind, we have compiled this list of biblical characteristics that we use to determine whether someone is qualified to serve on our top leadership team. In addition to the specific characteristics, I've provided some sample questions we consider as we review candidates.

• **Commitment to Christ** (1 Samuel 13:14; 1 Timothy 3:6; 1 Timothy 5:22). Are they fully devoted followers of Christ? Do they pursue Jesus passionately? Are they recent converts, or have they had time to prove that their faith is true?

• **Character** (1 Timothy 3:1-7; Titus 1:6-8). Do they possess solid character? For example, are they self-controlled? Are they gentle, hospitable, upright, holy, and disciplined?

• **Conduct** (1 Timothy 3:1-7; Titus 1:5-9). Do their actions reflect a full devotion to Christ? For example, are their marriages solid? Are they good parents? Are they quarrelsome and overbearing? Do they have a quick temper?

• **Comprehension** (Colossians 1:28-29; Titus 1:9). Do they have a good knowledge of God's Word? Are they able to defend the Christian faith and encourage people to take steps in spiritual maturity? Could they identify false doctrine? It's important to note here that 1 Timothy 5:17 suggests that not all elders are preachers and teachers. Just because someone serves on your senior leadership team doesn't necessarily mean you should put him or her in the pulpit on Sunday morning.

• **Capacity** (Acts 20:28; Hebrews 13:17). Do they reflect a concern for the spiritual well-being of the entire church, "all the flock," or just ministries or subministries within the church? Do they appreciate the responsibility and accountability God has given them to watch over the entire church?

• **Compassion** (Ezekiel 34; 1 Peter 5:2). Do they reflect a concern for helping lost people find Jesus? Do their hearts beat fast when discussing ministry opportunities to reach people who haven't heard about Christ?

• **Calling** (Galatians 1:1; Ephesians 1:1; 1 Peter 5:2). Do they consider the appointment to be from God or from men? Do they possess a clear sense that this is God's calling? Is it God's will?

In our church, it just so happens that each member of our Senior Management Team is also on staff. That doesn't necessarily need to be the case. In smaller churches, these same qualifications would apply to volunteer leaders serving on this team.

What matters most in making these decisions is that you're identifying people who can fulfill the spiritual and organizational leadership roles of your church. In our experience, we've asked someone to join this leadership team even though it didn't make sense on the organizational chart. Similarly, we've delayed adding leaders of significant ministry areas even though their roles might suggest they should be included.

Take time to consider these decisions carefully. Who you invite to participate on your leadership team will certainly influence your ministry's growth and the spiritual growth of your congregation. Pray for discernment. Give people time to prove their leadership potential. Talk to references. Talk about the decision with the rest of your leadership team. When the time is right, God will take you to your leader.

—Tony

53 People Give to Changed Lives

"Though they have been going through much trouble and hard times, their wonderful joy and deep poverty have overflowed in rich generosity" (2 Corinthians 8:2, NLT).

What motivates people to give? We pray for people to grow in their relationships with Christ, and it's through that maturity in faith that most people begin to understand the importance of biblical stewardship. Their giving ends up being a response to Jesus. But deep down, people also have a need to know how this offering is going to be used. They either want to see their gifts supporting ministries that positively influence people's lives or they want to see their contributions directly assisting people in need.

Because of that, we stopped including the budget and offering totals in our weekly bulletins a couple of years ago. It just wasn't helpful. People don't give to budgets. They're not motivated to make a tithe or offering by seeing that the church is several thousand dollars behind its budget. Budgets don't generate offerings.

People don't give to buildings, either. That's been our experience through the years. We've had multiple campaigns to take pledges for campus development, but we don't focus on constructing buildings. Instead, we talk about the people who will meet Jesus in the new space. We talk about the ministry to children and youth. We communicate the vision for how God may move and use our facility as a sanctuary for the poor, the hurting, the lonely, and the lost.

> People don't give to budgets. People don't give to buildings, either. People do give to changed lives.

People do give to changed lives. They give to a ministry that they know is having an impact on people's spiritual and physical well-being. They also give to vision. They want to know that the resources they provide will become an investment in life change. With that in mind, you need to routinely remind people how their giving is helping people meet Jesus, healing marriages, rescuing people from addictions, and offering new hope. In that way, giving truly becomes an act of worship.

Even with this said, there is an appropriate time for open and honest communication about the financial condition of your ministry. When you withhold that information and don't present it to the committed followers of Christ in your congregation, they may begin to raise questions about poor financial stewardship or, worse yet, mismanagement of resources. Your core needs to know when offerings aren't meeting ministry needs. Some will want to help. Most will want to pray with the leadership for wisdom about financial decisions and for God's provision and direction for the ministry. These situations offer great opportunities to talk about the many ways God has blessed your ministry in the past. You can also share what you're doing in the meantime to make ends meet. It's good for people to be reminded that you'll never outspend God's vision for your church. That message builds integrity and becomes the foundation for faithful giving to your ministry.

—Tony

5 The Low Bid May Cost More

Consider this scenario:

One Sunday morning everyone gathered in the auditorium, waiting for the service to begin. The pastor stood up for the normal announcement time. Typically, the announcements were too long and very boring. However, this time everyone tuned in as the pastor began, "I have something exciting to tell you today. Many of you have waited for this day for years. The elders have approved hiring a youth pastor." People applauded. He continued, "Here's how we'll do it: We will be accepting proposals from interested persons for the next thirty days. If you know someone who would like to be our youth pastor, please tell him or her to submit a proposal that includes exactly what he or she will accomplish and how much money he or she needs to do the job. We will then review all of the proposals, and we will choose the person who has agreed to the terms of the job for the least amount of money." The congregation was stunned.

Sounds absurd, right? No church would hire a youth pastor based on "low bid." Yet churches spend thousands, even millions, of dollars on buildings by choosing the contractors with the lowest bid. They assume that if the design documents are completely detailed, then anyone who submits a bid will give them the same exact end product as another bidder. So it comes down to money, right?

This is wrong. Very wrong. Like the hiring of a youth pastor, the hiring of a contractor requires you to look at more than just the bottom line. You must consider so many issues, including these:

• **Reputation.** What is the contractor's reputation with clients? with other contractors?

• **Honesty.** Do the owners, project managers, and superintendents exhibit integrity and honesty? Are they true to their word? Or do they deliberately submit low bids, knowing they will make it up later with change orders?

• **Affinity.** Do you like them? Do you have a connection with those you'll be working with day to day?

- **Workmanship.** What is the quality of their work? Do they cut corners? Do they hide mistakes?
- **Ownership.** Do they use the cheapest materials when they can get away with it? Do they treat your building as if it were their own?

The only way to answer these questions is to conduct interviews and reference checks as thoroughly as you would with potential employees. Do this religiously, and you will save yourself much heartache. Skip this advice, and you can start taking the Tums today.

Every time I have seen a church choose the low bid, problems have surfaced later. My dad used to say, "You get what you pay for." I told him he shouldn't end a sentence with a preposition, but nevertheless, his point was valid. It's true that, most times, the low bid will cost you more in the long run than the right bid.

—Tim

55 Attend the Innovative Church Conference Every Year

This is more than just an unsolicited plug for the very best church conference in all the country, hosted annually by Granger Community Church. Let's face it. Where else can you go to experience challenging teaching, phenomenal music, and cutting-edge media, while at the same time enjoying the tropical northern-Indiana climate that makes South Bend a vacation destination for throngs of people each year? What? You say it's too cold for you sissy pastors in Florida and Southern California? Like God really calls anyone to take up the cross and follow him in locations like that. Northern Indiana—that's where *real ministry* takes place.

Actually, I share the opportunity to come to our conference to encourage you to invest in training for both your staff and volunteers. We're constantly sending our team off to learn from others. That includes church leadership conferences. It also includes ministry-specific opportunities at various workshops and seminars. We try to take advantage of training opportunities that are offered in our immediate area, but we've also budgeted for trips across the country to participate in the best continuing education that's available. If you've identified the right staff members and volunteers, they're going to want to attend training events to improve their skills, to be challenged to broaden their vision, and to network with the best and brightest from other ministry teams.

At Granger, we spend about 5 percent of payroll on staff training, retreats, and professional expense accounts used to encourage employee development. We spend several thousand dollars on top of that to help volunteers take time off work and experience training opportunities beyond what we can provide on our own campus.

In addition to providing new skills,

Visiting other church conferences really stretches our vision for what God might have in store for our ministry.

visiting other church conferences really stretches our vision for what God might have in store for our ministry. It's tough to walk on the campus of North Point Community Church (www.northpoint.org) or Fellowship Church (www.fellowshipchurch.com), for example, and not dream about the future of our church. Even if I've heard the same principles previously, I know I always have at least a dozen take-aways that affect how I approach ministry. Additionally, it's just one more way to experience life together as a team.

Your staff and volunteers are your most important asset. That suggests they should also be the primary place you invest your financial resources.

I know what you're thinking. It just might be time to book those airline tickets to South Bend. If your curiosity is piqued, check out the additional details about the Innovative Church Conference and other resources to equip church leaders on page 207. If you come, we'll give you a big Hoosier welcome and tell you all we know about growing a church and helping people take their next step toward Christ.

—Tony

56 Read Your Comment Cards

If yours is a growing church, you are likely designing a weekend service to reach a certain target. Whoever your target is and whatever your purpose is, don't you want to know if you are being effective? Don't you want to know if something isn't working? Don't you want to know if there are distractions that are counterproductive to your purpose?

Recently I heard a talk by Daniel Goleman, author of *Emotional Intelligence*. He shared the example of a restaurant owner who wanted true, unfiltered feedback from his customers. The owner said, "I can't walk around the dining room and ask my customers how they are enjoying their meals." Why? "Because they all lie to me and tell me what I want to hear." So he sorted through the trash can at the end of each day to see what people were leaving on their plates. That's some pretty effective feedback.

At every service at Granger, we include a reply card in the program titled "Tell Us About Your Experience Today." It includes several lines for people to describe the good and bad of their visit. Whether the card is signed or anonymous, we read every response.

Here are some things we've learned through these cards that we wouldn't otherwise have known:

• One set of doors wasn't getting unlocked before the services. (Seems like a good thing to know.)

• One of our lawn sprinklers was aimed wrong and was spraying in car windows on Sunday morning. (We probably should fix that.)

• The volume is too loud. (There is always someone who thinks the volume is too loud or too soft, but if we get a number of comments from the same service, then it's probably something we should adjust.)

• Someone wrote, "You seem to talk about Jesus a lot." (We know we are reaching our target!)

Whatever your system is, figure out a way to get some honest feedback from your people. Take to heart what needs to be addressed and forget the rest.

—Tim

57 Bake Sales Don't Pay the Water Bill

They're well-meaning people. The conversations usually start out with a comment such as "I have an idea that could really help the church." I usually get a couple of these calls each month. We've had car salesmen who want to give a percentage of each sale to the church in exchange for advertising in the bulletin. We've had insurance people wanting to sell whole-life policies benefiting the church. There have been people wanting to offer credit cards, investment plans, and newspapers supported by advertising businesses within the church. The list could go on and on.

We don't do any of this at Granger. There are no bake sales, no car washes, and no raffles. The only thing we do that comes remotely close to this is a "Save Your Change" campaign the youth ministry holds each year to provide scholarship support for youth mission trips. Even that really isn't a fundraiser because people are making a financial contribution directly to our church to support ongoing ministry. The financial contribution just happens to be in the form of accumulated loose change.

> **Here's what we do instead of fundraising: We encourage people to make tithes and offerings.**

Here's what we do instead of fundraising: We encourage people to make tithes and offerings. It's pretty simple. We tell people what we think God wants our church to accomplish. We teach biblical stewardship principles. People give their offerings. Then we develop specific ministry plans based on the resources God provides. If money isn't available, we tell people what areas of ministry will have to wait until the financial resources are available to fund those priorities.

Here's what that strategic decision accomplishes. It keeps the message clear and focused. The emphasis is on helping people understand biblical stewardship principles. Instead of standing up on Sunday asking people to get their cars washed, the pastor's teaching people how to worship God through the act of sacrificial giving.

Additionally, this helps people focus on serving God through ministry involvement. Fundraisers are time consuming. If people are focused on selling something at your church, they aren't focused on serving Jesus. If people are talking about their products, they aren't telling people about Jesus.

More important, eliminating fundraisers creates a better environment for new people who are connecting to your church. You don't want newcomers to be bombarded by salespeople. Instead, they need an environment in which they can meet Jesus and learn how to take steps in that relationship.

Ban the bake sales, and focus on biblical stewardship. In the end, your ministry will be stronger, and your people will be a few pounds lighter.

—Tony

58 Your Organizational Structure Should Change Often

"Most of what we call management consists of making it difficult for people to get their work done."
—attributed to Peter Drucker, in *Service America! Doing Business in the New Economy*, by Karl Albrecht and Ron Zemke

When you look at the inner workings of many churches, you might think that the structures were put in place to make it as difficult as possible to get anything done. Or maybe the structures were established to give power-hungry people meetings to attend so they could look and feel important. Or perhaps the structures were designed to keep the pastor hyper-accountable so he wouldn't step out of line.

However, the sole purpose of structure in a healthy church is to facilitate ministry. The questions should be, "What minimal structure is necessary to offer wise counsel and appropriate accountability? What will provide a quick, clear path for fulfilling our mission as a church?"

There is no prescribed fix-all structure that can be dropped in place in any given church. Furthermore, the "perfect" organizational structure that you implement today probably won't work in a few years. The church is a living organism and is always changing and growing. The structure that facilitates that growth should be regularly evaluated to make sure it is still helping, not hindering, the ministry.

At Granger, we went through this process most recently in 1999. Our attendance had grown from four hundred to fifteen hundred in only five

Granger has gone through three major structural changes and many minor adjustments.
• **1986:** The church held its first services. A steering committee composed of area pastors and businessmen met weekly. Financial checks required signatures of two accountants who didn't attend the church.
• **1989:** A lay board of church members was developed. They met weekly, with the senior pastor, and handled all day-to-day decisions of the church.
• **1993:** The board relinquished day-to-day decisions to the staff, but continued to drive the direction and hire staff.
• **1999:** The board now just protects mission, vision, and values. All ministry direction and operational decisions are assumed by hired staff.

years. We had lay people with full-time jobs who were giving up several nights a month to make decisions about the direction and operations of the church. It took hours to get them up to speed so they could make informed decisions. It was a waste of their time, and it was slowing down ministry. They had no time left to be involved in ministry because we were using it to make decisions. These were the same decisions that the hired staff could have made on their own. You can imagine everyone's relief when we recommended a new structure that would value their time. We began bringing them in only for the truly important discussions: reviewing the mission of the church or interviewing a candidate for a senior position. We left administrative and operational discussions to those we had hired to make such decisions.

I'm sure that we'll need to change our structure again within a few years. With annual growth averaging about 24 percent, we are doubling in size every three years. However, we have a church culture in which no one will be surprised or frustrated when we walk in with another recommended change.

Change is a part of our DNA.

—Tim

59 Ministry Should Be Fun

"A man can do nothing better than to eat and drink and find satisfaction in his work. This too, I see, is from the hand of God" (Ecclesiastes 2:24).

Around Granger, we've developed a culture that promotes fun. People encourage one another. They laugh. Everyone's positive. I've worked in other environments, so I know this is unusual. But it's part of the fabric of Granger Community Church.

Never underestimate the power of your attitude in influencing your church's culture.

A lot of that stems from the leadership of our senior pastor, Mark Beeson. I've heard it said that the church takes on the personality of the senior pastor, and that's most likely the case here. Mark is the world's greatest encourager. As a result, people around him experience a lot of joy. Never underestimate the power of your attitude in influencing your church's culture.

In addition to Mark's influence, we've done some things to intentionally make ministry life more fun. Here's a list of the types of activities members of the staff do together every month or so.

• We periodically eat lunch together to celebrate a variety of events.

• We play together in activities such as go-cart racing and putt-putt golf.

• We attend movies together.

• We have a Christmas dinner each year that includes spouses and a white-elephant gift exchange.

• We have an annual retreat for planning, training, and plenty of free time for fun activities together.

• We attend conferences together to learn new ministry ideas and to hang out and reconnect with the others on the team.

Not only do we do this with our staff team, we also encourage ministry leaders to creatively promote fun activities within their ministry teams. We specifically budget money for people to build fun into their agendas.

Why do we do this? For one thing, it makes going to work every day a lot easier. But there are other benefits. A fun ministry environment encourages people to be creative and take risks. It develops an inviting atmosphere for newcomers. Lost people would rather hang out with positive people than with condemning, hardhearted folks. It encourages people to volunteer to serve. People want to join in the fun.

Yes, ministry is hard work. It involves long hours. Sometimes relationships get messy. But I'm convinced that God wants us to enjoy our ministry experience. As with Paul, we can expect persecution and suffering, but we can also choose to take delight in these difficulties, knowing that God gives us strength in our weaknesses. Your attitude matters, so choose to have fun!

—Tony

60 It Could Take Twice as Long but Shouldn't Cost Twice as Much

There is a common belief about construction that I've heard repeated a thousand times: "Every construction project takes twice as long and costs twice as much as you think it will."

I remember our first building project. I told the group confidently, "It will be done by Christmas." Deane was in the group. He was older, wiser, and much more experienced than I. He pulled me aside afterward and said, "Be careful how confidently you give deadlines. Stuff happens. This project probably won't be done until after Easter, and you don't want to get people's hopes up too much."

I thanked him for his counsel but arrogantly set out to prove him wrong. Deane was right. We didn't move into the new facility until August, and I learned a valuable lesson.

Although it didn't take twice as long as planned, it did take a lot longer than expected. He was right; "stuff" happens. In our case, a nationwide shortage of steel brought the project to a standstill for thirteen weeks. That drove us into the winter months, and we had to wait for a thaw. Stuff happens. Three of our four projects have been completed later than we would have liked.

However, when it comes to money, it shouldn't cost twice as much. At Granger, we have completed four major and several minor construction projects totaling nearly $10 million. *All of them have been completed under budget.* Many church leaders have asked us, "What is the secret to ending under budget?" Here are some simple strategies for keeping your project's budget in check:

• *Never* **start the project until you have received a Guaranteed Maximum Price (GMP) from your contractor.** This is crucial. It should be in writing and included in a signed contract.

• *Always* **include a contingency amount over and above your contractor's GMP.** Typically, I plan on 10 percent over and above the contract. This is a part of the project budget, but it is *not* added to the contract at the beginning of the project. It is money that is earmarked

128

to add to the contract later, if needed, for change orders or over-sights. This contingency might be used to cover minor errors in the blueprints. Or, if you near the end of the project and you have contingency funds remaining, then you can release the funds for items that you had to reduce or eliminate earlier.

• *always* **require that every change order is submitted in a timely fashion in writing.** Include this requirement in your contract. Keep an ongoing list of change orders so you always know how much of the contingency fund is available.

• *always* **identify an individual who is solely responsible for the project, and make sure your contractor knows who that is.** Our senior pastor made it clear to the contractors before the first project began by stating, "Tim is in charge. If you get direction from anyone else, including me, ignore it. Tim will be the only person from the church giving you direction." If many people are making changes, then costs will get out of hand.

Plan more time for the project than the contractor tells you is needed. It takes time to produce a quality project. But manage the costs well, and you will be heralded by your church—and, I believe, by Jesus—for being a wise steward of the money entrusted to you.

—Tim

61 If You Can't Pay Your Employees Well, You Have Too Many Employees

> "If you think we're wax-works," he said, "you ought to pay, you know. Wax-works weren't made to be looked at for nothing. Nohow!"
> —*Through the Looking Glass* by Lewis Carroll

Or maybe the gospel according to Tweedledum and Tweedledee should read, "If you think we're pastors, you ought to pay. Pastors weren't made to be looked at for nothing." In fact, the Bible teaches fairly clearly in several passages that leaders of the church should be financially supported by the church. For example, consider this: "Elders who do their work well should be paid well, especially those who work hard at both preaching and teaching. For the Scripture says, 'Do not keep an ox from eating as it treads out the grain.' And in another place, 'Those who work deserve their pay!' " (1 Timothy 5:17-18, NLT).

Now, before you start trying to calculate what Tweedledee and I make, let me just say that we try to pay all of our staff just slightly above the average wage level when compared to other churches our size. If you're wondering how much churches pay, don't start calling other pastors. They really shouldn't be sharing that information. Instead, there are a number of organizations that publish salary surveys that you can use to compare wage levels with other churches of your size and in similar locations. Here are some organizations that publish this type of information:

• National Association of Church Business Administration (www.nacba.net)

• Christian Management Association (www.cmaonline.org)

• Leadership Network (www.leadnet.org)

At Granger, we've avoided equal, across-the-board wage increases and have opted to reward employees based on their performance and ministry capacity. So we're not only making external comparisons with other churches and local organizations, we're also making internal comparisons based on ministry roles. Whatever your formula, you need to make sure your staff is being paid appropriately. If you can't pay your employees well, you have too many employees.

We've entered every budget year with this decision to make: Do we add a new position that we desperately need, or do we give members of our current staff the salary increases they deserve? At Granger, nine times out of ten, we choose the wage increase. The only time we haven't is when we've determined, with the input of current staff, that the health of our team will be jeopardized if we don't move forward with new additions.

If you're looking for places to save money, staff salaries and benefits shouldn't be the first place you look. Make sure your compensation plans are consistent with biblical guidelines. Your staff won't get wealthy in ministry, but they should be "paid well" to allow them to focus on serving Jesus and the church without dealing with personal financial concerns.

It's Tweedledee, not Tweedle-free, and we weren't made to be looked at for nothing.

—Tony

62 Avoid These Classic Communication Blunders

Communication is an art. It takes careful planning and years of practice to become a good communicator. I know of many churches in which the pastor is good at preaching or teaching but has difficulty communicating the addition of a service, the resignation of a staff member, or the disappointing delay of a building project. And yet these are the big issues in the life of a church that tend to divide or cause conflict if not handled delicately. Many church leaders make one or more of the following classic communication blunders.

• **They communicate *too little*.** When this happens, the members or key leaders who have invested their lives in the church have no idea what's going on! Rumors start to circulate and, in the absence of correct information, people believe what they hear.

• **They communicate *too much*.** In this situation, people get tired of hearing about it. You'll hear people say, "That's all the church talks about!"

• **They communicate to the *wrong people*.** Rather than targeting their communication to select groups (such as newcomers, new members, charter members, or leaders), they use the church platform to speak to the general crowd. As a result, some people are bored, and others feel the information is too general.

• **They communicate the *wrong information*.** In the case of a building project, they may spend too much time on construction terms and details rather than casting vision for the changed lives their new space will embrace. Face it: Not everyone is excited about blueprints.

Three basic principles will help you avoid these mistakes. First, be aware of the mistakes. Keep in front of you a list of the four blunders described above. Second, figure out an effective system for obtaining feedback from your people. This allows you to know the kinds of questions "real people" are asking. Third, determine your target groups, and design communication unique to each group. Here are some examples:

• **Newcomers.** With this group, emphasize vision. Talk about changed lives. In most cases, they don't want or need details.

• **Staff and key leaders.** This group needs to know details. Tell them what is happening, when it will happen, and how it will benefit the church. They should know how it will affect them and their ministry areas. Since they will be answering questions from others, help them know how to best communicate the information.

• **Donors.** You may be talking about a project that certain people helped fund, such as a missions trip. You could send weekly e-mail updates letting these people know the status of the trip and relaying stories about how lives have changed as a result of their investment.

> Always keep the vision in front of your people.

Next, be honest about changes or delays. People expect difficulties—they just don't want the problems to be hidden from them.

And finally, always keep the vision in front of your people. Tie every project, every event, and every change to the bottom line: "It's about people. It's about changed lives."

—Tim

63 Don't Let the Treasurer Decide How to Spend the Money

Obviously, any ministry trying to maintain integrity with the resources God has provided will establish certain procedures for handling the offering, counting it, making purchases, budgeting, and other tasks involving money. As churches pursue audited financial statements, your auditors are also going to note the need for these controls. As you are putting appropriate controls in place, make sure your treasurer understands his or her role. This may sound counterintuitive, but don't let the treasurer decide how to spend the money.

The people who cut the checks and handle the money should never have decision-making authority for purchases made in your church. They should implement systems adopted by the leadership team. They should create helpful financial reports and monitor the financial condition of the ministry. They should *not* decide if it's OK to purchase a new keyboard for your band or more pencils for your secretaries. Unfortunately, there are too many churches out there where the church treasurer, or the "controller," is the person who's actually controlling what's happening or not happening in the ministry because he or she controls the purse strings. Your board should set the overall ministry budget, and the senior pastor or the senior management team should always maintain strategic decision-making authority for financial decisions.

Our senior pastor has shared the story of Alice, the treasurer of a church he once served. She kept all of the financial records and the checkbook in a shoe box, and then hid the shoe box in a closet to make sure no one found it. Alice truly was a controller.

This principle also applies to personnel decisions. As the church grows and adds staff or identifies lay leaders in the human resources area, these people should not make final decisions regarding hiring and firing. The human resources area can assist with the recruitment and selection process, provide guidance when handling discipline issues, create methods for monitoring performance, help establish pay systems, and coordinate benefit programs. It shouldn't decide who becomes your new youth pastor. That, once again, is the job of the senior pastor or the senior staff leader over that ministry area.

In both of these capacities—finance and human resources—the primary function is to facilitate ministry, not to decide what will or won't happen within the ministry.

Let me add one side note here for senior pastors. As your church grows, the senior pastor and other senior staff leaders will begin to delegate finance and human resources functions to others in the organization. Even as that happens, the senior staff leaders in the organization must still keep abreast of and be involved in these critical ministry decisions. Even though you may not have the skills or passion to be an expert in these areas, you can't completely abrogate these responsibilities. Ultimately, your name and the integrity of your entire ministry are in your hands. If something blows up in the area of finances or personnel, people are going to look straight to the top. The buck stops in the pulpit.

—Tony

64 Believe the Best

Consider this scenario. You are an elder at your church. You receive a letter that accuses your pastor of having an illicit affair. The letter is not signed. What do you do?

First, consider character. Before you show the letter to anyone, ask yourself, "Is this plausible?" Does this accusation confirm any thoughts you've had about the pastor? Or is it entirely unbelievable?

Next, evaluate the source. If it is anonymous and there is no reason to believe there could be any truth to it, ignore it. Let your pastor know about the letter and that you are ignoring it. This will reaffirm your trust in his or her leadership and integrity. Believe the best.

If it is anonymous, but it kind of makes sense, then ask questions. If you believe there is something about your pastor's character, schedule, or activity that makes you believe it could be true, you should sit down with your pastor, look into his or her eyes, and ask the tough questions. Ask him or her to prove, if possible, that it could not be true. When the conversation is over, believe the best.

> Just because there are two different stories doesn't mean someone is intentionally lying.

If the source is not anonymous, then consider the source. What is the person's record? his reputation? her motive? What does he have to gain? What does she have to lose? While asking these questions, believe the best of your pastor.

As you examine the allegation, remember the following important principles:

• Don't expect to find "the truth." Everyone has a different side to the same story. Each perspective has been filtered through moods, baggage, emotions, experience, and knowledge. Just because there are two different stories doesn't mean someone is intentionally lying.

• If the accusation involves physical or sexual abuse of a child, then you must deal with it even if it is anonymous. Talk to the accused person to discern if there is any validity to the accusation. While you are in the fact-finding phase, remove the person from any contact with children. This is for both the safety of the kids *and* the legal protection of the church. Do this very quickly, because if the individual is innocent you'll want to quickly declare your confidence in his or her integrity to those who know about the accusation.

• If the accusation is about nonsexual, noncriminal sins (such as bad business ethics, lying, gossip, a bad temper, or drinking), then use a "teaching moment" to help the individual who is making the accusation. Let him or her know that your church is full of sinners with baggage from bad decisions and broken relationships. Say things such as, "Isn't it exciting that we have a church in which broken people can worship and serve while they're putting their lives back together?"

Through it all, believe the best. Handle the discovery phase quickly, and believe the best.

—Tim

65 Create a Culture That Expects Volunteers to Do It Before Staff

"Their responsibility is to equip God's people to do his work and build up the church, the body of Christ" (Ephesians 4:12, NLT).

One way to stop ministry from taking place in your church is to hire someone to do something every time a task must be completed. In order for growth to take place in your church, you need to empower volunteers to do the ministry. You should hire people to do only what unpaid servants can't accomplish. Your church will never have enough money to hire people to fill every key ministry role.

In October 2002, Granger had over eighteen hundred people connected in some form of ministry, either through small groups or through task teams. That's over fifty percent of our weekend attendance who were connected to ministry and relationships. With only thirty-five full-time-equivalent employees on staff, our attendance growth would have stalled long ago had we not released ministry to lay people.

One key example of this is our children's ministry. On any given weekend at Granger, we have nearly a thousand children from birth through fifth grade and the equivalent of only three people on staff. Obviously these three people can't come close to touching the lives of these kids on their own. Instead, we have 255 active volunteers in the children's area who serve from week to week. These volunteers have grown accustomed to our practice of encouraging people to attend one service and serve during a second service.

Some volunteers check children in. Some are involved in preparing art projects, music, and dramas. Others provide care for our children as they form small groups. Some volunteers teach. Several key lay people oversee entire age groups in significant leadership roles. There are many other volunteer roles as well.

So what do the three children's staff people do? They are the vision champions. They make sure the children's ministry team is focused on fulfilling the mission of our church. They build teams and equip volunteers to carry out the ministry.

We've implemented this model throughout the rest of our ministry. It's a simple strategy. Volunteers need to do it first.

—Tony

66 Read the Bible and Fast Company Magazine

That's right—read the Bible *and* Fast Company magazine.

Not at the same time.

Not for the same length of time.

Not with the same trust of the authors.

Not with the same value of the content.

Nevertheless, make sure your reading is diverse.

Have you ever met a pastor who is "so heavenly minded that he is of no earthly good"? These pastors can quote lots of Scripture but can't carry on a conversation with a gas station attendant or a waitress at a restaurant. They spend 100 percent of their time with church people, engaged in church conversation, studying the Bible, reading Christian magazines or books by Christian authors, preparing messages, and going to Christian conferences. They have no connection to the real world!

Of course you should read the Bible every day. All the things these pastors do are good. But you should also spend some of your time reading material that will prepare you to reach your culture. Find some secular books or magazines that have the *best practices* of the world, and learn what you can to help lead your church more effectively.

Here are some good secular books and magazines that we've found helpful.

Magazines

Fast Company (www.fastcompany.com)
Wired (www.wired.com/wired/)
Red Herring (www.redherring.com)
Business 2.0 (www.business2.com)

Books

Built to Last by Jim Collins and Jerry Porras
Organizing Genius by Warren Bennis and Patricia Biederman
The Effective Executive by Peter Drucker

The 21 Irrefutable Laws of Leadership by John Maxwell
Leading Change by John Kotter

You can also learn much from newspapers, movies, novels, and television.

There are two primary reasons for augmenting your spiritual study with secular reading and viewing. The first is that you'll actually learn stuff that can help your church. There are principles from the world about innovation, creativity, financial management, and growing an organization that translate well to the church. Second, you'll be experiencing what many of your people are reading and watching. You'll be able to stay abreast of the terminology and changes in the business world and our culture, and you'll be able to relate to many in your unchurched community.

"I read about eight newspapers in a day. When I'm in a town with only one newspaper, I read it eight times."
—Will Rogers

—Tim

67 Your Structure Should Mirror Your Strategy

Many ministry strategies are used in churches throughout the country. These strategies provide a defined process for helping people move from being nonbelievers to being fully devoted followers of Jesus Christ. Willow Creek Community Church (www.willowcreek.org) has a seven-step strategy. Saddleback Church (www.saddleback.com) uses the five purposes—membership, maturity, ministry, missions, and magnification. Andy Stanley's church (www.northpoint.org) helps people move from the "foyer" to the "living room" to the "kitchen." The specific strategy isn't what's important, but having a strategy is.

Without a process to help people take steps in their faith journey, the church tends to structure around programs or the strengths of the senior pastor. It then becomes difficult to achieve health and balance. Until about five years ago, that's what we did at Granger. We were effectively attracting a crowd on the weekends, but there was no clearly defined path to help people mature in their faith. We decided to implement the Purpose Driven Church model (www.purposedriven.com), and this change transformed our ministry. For the very first time we identified a clear path to help people take their next steps toward Christ.

Once you've identified your discipleship strategy, make sure your structure reflects that paradigm. Here's how Granger generally structures some of the key ministry teams that support each component of our strategy.

Creative Arts
- Worship (bands, vocalists, and dance)
- Drama
- Technical (media, lighting, audio, and cameras)

Life Missions
- Evangelism training
- Local missions (homeless shelter, Habitat for Humanity, etc.)
- Cross-cultural missions

Operations
- Finance
- Campus operations
- Technology and communications
- Human resources
- Office management

Connections

- "First Impressions" (ushers, greeters, traffic, and information center)
- Small groups
- Ministry connections
- Community care (weddings, funerals, hospital visitation, and prayer)
- Counseling
- "Next Step Resources" (bookstore and café)
- Baptism

Life Development

- Children's ministry (birth through fifth grade)
- Middle school ministry
- High school ministry

WiredChurches —ministry to other church leaders

- Innovative Church Conference
- Seminars and workshops
- Campus tours
- Resource development

If you're familiar with the Purpose Driven model, you may notice a couple of key areas that aren't as well defined in our staffing structure. Right now one of our pastors oversees both "missions" and "maturity" while another one focuses on "membership" and "ministry." Of course, we have key lay leaders supporting all of these areas in more specific roles. As we continue to grow and resources become available, we'll begin to distinguish those roles further and assign one staff leader to champion each purpose in our ministry strategy. The other option smaller churches have is identifying high-capacity volunteer leaders to oversee the primary components of their discipleship strategies.

Before you fill your next key ministry role, whether volunteer or paid staff, step back and take a look at how your ministry teams are organized. Make sure your structure mirrors your strategy.

—Tony

68 Design the Biggest Lobby You Think You'll Need, Then Double It

When you begin designing a building, everyone will try to talk you out of wide hallways and a big lobby. Here's my advice: Don't listen to them. Nod your head and smile, but ignore them.

Architects, contractors, and consultants have all told us we're crazy to have such wide hallways and such a large lobby. They've said that it's a waste of space. They've said that it's "bigger than code requires." They've told us that we will lose valuable space in our auditorium or classrooms by putting so much space in our hallways.

However, we have worked to convince them that our value for the hallways and lobby is equal to our value for the classrooms and auditorium space. We believe that if people have a bad experience in either space, then they may not come back!

Here are some arguments you can use to convince your designers of your need for wide hallways and a big lobby:

• Connecting with people and building relationships are part of your mission. You want people to do this, and providing the space allows it to happen.

Plan to accommodate two crowds at a time in your building.

• A single mom often struggles by herself to get her children to their classrooms. Even an average-sized woman is rather wide when carrying an infant seat and a toddler. With one or two more children walking beside her, she needs plenty of space.

• You want your newcomers to have a good experience from the minute they drive onto your property until they leave. If they have to squeeze through crowded hallways and endure close proximity with strangers, they may not return.

• Even if you're not offering multiple services now, you may be in the future. That means you should plan to accommodate two crowds at a time in your building. You'll have a full crowd that has just attended a service; these folks are picking up their children and making their way to the parking lot. At the same time, a new crowd of people are parking their cars and trying to work their way into your building to drop off their kids and enjoy the next service.

When your mission is to connect people to meaningful relationships, you need to provide the space that allows that to happen. Wide hallways and a big lobby can do that. So, even if you have to "lobby" for a big lobby, don't give up until you win.

—Tim

69 Money Management Matters

"This silver and gold is a freewill offering to the Lord, the God of our ancestors. Guard these treasures well until you present them, without an ounce lost, to the leading priests, the Levites, and the leaders of Israel at the storerooms of the Lord's temple in Jerusalem" (Ezra 8:28b-29, NLT).

> People don't give money because of good financial management, but they'll stop giving without it.

You are responsible for every dollar God provides for your ministry. No matter how many people are in your congregation, you can't overlook the need to maintain integrity with these financial resources. People don't give money because of good financial management, but they'll stop giving without it.

At Granger, we send a letter to people after they've made their first contribution. We thank them for their offerings and reiterate our commitment to use their gifts to further the mission to which God has called our church. In it we include this paragraph, highlighting some of the steps we've taken to manage these financial resources wisely: "At Granger Community Church, we do all we can to maintain the highest level of integrity with the resources God gives us through the tithes and offerings of people like you. Examples of steps we've taken include establishing policies for secure handling and counting of weekly offerings, preparing an annual budget that is reviewed and approved by a separate board of lay people, and conducting an annual outside audit by an accounting firm to review all our financial records and controls."

You'll notice that we annually ask an outside accounting firm to perform an audit. As your church approaches $500,000 in annual receipts, this is a step you may want to consider. Smaller churches still have a responsibility to annually review their financial condition and controls. However, rather than hiring an outside firm, those churches could identify someone from the church who has accounting or bookkeeping experience but isn't serving the church in a financial role. Some churches may have two or three people who could perform the internal audit as a team. You could also consider partnering with another local church to have each treasurer review the other church's books.

Whether you do an internal financial review or hire an outside firm to perform an audit, here are some basic steps you should take to protect your ministry.

- **Designated gifts.** Establish a policy to make sure contributions that are received for a specific purpose are used in the way they were intended.

- **Counting offerings.** Two unrelated people should count your offerings, and these teams should rotate whenever possible.

- **Separation of duties.** Your purchasing policies should prevent the same person from approving expenditures, preparing the checks, and signing the checks.

- **Reconciliation.** Somebody should make sure the bank statements are reconciled each month and confirm the accuracy of financial statements.

Make every effort to put financial controls, reporting, and regular communications in place so there is no hint of financial impropriety in your church. Even the *perception* that something is wrong can derail a healthy ministry.

—Tony

70 Plan for Negative Press

It will happen.

It could be ugly.

It might set your church back years.

A crisis. A major crisis of significant proportions. Go ahead...imagine what it might be. It's worse than that.

It's the stuff that news reporters love. It's the scoop they want to deliver before anyone else finds out. It's the stuff people love to read.

You may think your church is exempt. You may think that focusing on holiness and integrity and preaching the Bible somehow makes you immune. You may say with pride, "We've never had a sexual sin within our leadership." Be careful, though, because people are human. And Satan is alive. It will happen. It's just a matter of time.

You must prepare now. You must develop good rapport with reporters and news anchors in your community so good relationships are already established when the negative press hits.

At Granger, it took sixteen years. And when it happened, it was big and it was messy. It could have been devastating for our church and the community. However, we had been preparing for crisis for years through our interactions with the news media.

Here are ways to prepare for a crisis:

• **Keep a list of reporters** from every TV, radio, and news outlet in your community.

• **Let them know every time something positive is happening at your church.** Official press releases are fine, but making personal calls to encourage them to see the event, outreach, or new ministry keeps the relationships strong. Do this especially when you have a ministry that is helping the community (Habitat for Humanity, work with the underprivileged, and helping youth, for example). Build a relationship with them. Don't ever be mean, cynical, or condescending toward them.

• **Stay tuned in to that reporter.** When reporters write a compelling article or deliver a great interview, jot them a note congratulating them on a job well done. (Do you know how often they get critical letters, and how rarely they get letters of thanks?)

• **When the crisis hits and they call the church, never say, "No comment."** Invite them to come and sit down with you. Let them see the personal side, where you're experiencing the pain. Don't limit their understanding to a copy of the "official statement." And remember, nothing you say is ever off the record. Nothing.

During our crisis, the major newspapers and television reporters in the area chose not to run the story. One small community newspaper wrote an article three weeks after the fact about how the church was caring for the family of the individual involved. I believe the response of the media was in large part due to the relationship we had developed with the news community.

Prepare now for the crisis. Follow these suggestions, and maybe the crisis won't be so big.

—Tim

71 Your Web Strategy Involves More Than Launching a Web Site

I was made for this generation. While sitting at my computer in the comfort of my home office, I can pay my bills, purchase a new book, check the weather, make sure the Fighting Irish pulled out another victory, converse with my mom via instant messaging, access my church computer files, track the delivery of my book, listen to the most recent smooth jazz releases, send messages throughout the world, and praise God every day for Bill Gates. I love the twenty-first century!

Here's what I also know to be true—there are lots of people just like me. We do our research on the Internet. We do our shopping on the Internet. We manage all our investments and banking on the Internet. We handle much of our communications on the Internet. Believe it or not, we even select churches on the Internet. Scary, isn't it?

> We need to be creating opportunities for people to do anything online that they would typically do within the four walls of our church buildings.

The Web isn't just about sharing information—although that's one of its important functions. The Web is also about interaction. People can learn and respond on the Web. They can ask questions and get answers. In tomorrow's church, people may not even have to set foot on your campus. They'll be able to listen to a message, download worship music, communicate with their e-group, study additional resources, share prayer requests, make their offerings, and take their next Bible classes online. In your online coffeehouse, they may even select their favorite reading room to browse new books, listen to their favorite music, and chat with friends while sipping coffee they've ordered online from your church's café.

A Web strategy involves far more than just launching a Web site. We need to be creating opportunities for people to do anything online that they would typically do within the four walls of our church buildings. We need to provide methods for signing up for classes *and* taking classes. We need to create systems that allow people to update their own mailing addresses, review their giving records, and communicate with their ministry leaders. We need to integrate what's happening on the Web with what's happening in the church database, classrooms, and sanctuary. I don't believe the Internet can replace buildings and all the interactions and ministry that transpire in those locations, but it can certainly empower ministries by automating processes while at the same time adding to the "experience" that our culture craves.

We live 24/7 with the world at our fingertips. The Internet is here to stay. Let's make the best use of technology to reach our communities for Jesus Christ.

—Tony

72 Teach Others What You Are Learning

I've heard a new term in recent years. People will say, "Granger Community Church is a *teaching church*." This term indicates that we are intentionally holding conferences and doing what we can to help other churches learn and grow. It's true that we try to look at everything we do in light of how it could help other churches. *Teaching church* is a pretty good description of one of our values.

However, I have a problem with this term. Why isn't every church in the world a teaching church? Why doesn't every church of 100 look for ways to help churches of 50? Why doesn't every church of 250 look for ways to help churches of 100? Why doesn't every church of 500 look for ways to help churches of 250? Why doesn't every church of 1,000 look for ways to help churches of 500?

Many churches are starting to catch on. Ten years ago, if you wanted to attend a conference at a church that was getting the job done, you had fewer than ten choices. Today there are scores. More and more churches are wanting to help resource other churches in any way they can.

At Granger, we've written it right into our vision. One of our major points states, *"Resourcing the Church: We will enthusiastically give our resources, experience, and giftedness to train and encourage those intent on building prevailing churches."*

There is not a church in the world that can't be a teacher to another church. You may have just started one month ago and have only twelve people coming to your services. Guess what? Even you can help pastors who are thinking about starting a church!

Even if your church is small and it seems as if you have nothing to offer, there is something that your church does well. Other churches could benefit from your expertise and knowledge. Figure out what that is, and determine to offer your learnings to other churches. If you are just now launching a new church, then cast the vision with your new members that your church will always offer help to other churches. Build it into your church's culture!

—Tim

73

Handle Tough Situations Head-On

"If anyone is causing divisions among you, give a first and second warning. After that, have nothing more to do with that person" (Titus 3:10, NLT).

Police departments across the country have policies in place to help officers know how to respond when they confront uncooperative people. It's called a continuum of force. After evaluating the circumstances, a police officer will implement various tactics to handle combative or noncompliant individuals. Officers know that any situation will require constant evaluation to determine when additional force is needed. They also know that, after considering the facts and circumstances, they have the freedom to skip steps in the continuum when warranted. Because they've learned how to use appropriate force in any given situation, police officers are able to respond without hesitation. Once a decision is made, they are committed to properly executing that tactic.

In ministry, there is a similar continuum that leaders must also learn and practice. Instead of force, this is a continuum of care. These biblical guidelines are detailed in various passages of the Bible including Matthew 18; 1 Corinthians 5; 2 Corinthians 13; and Titus 3. Here's what the continuum of care looks like:

• **Coaching session.** This is a one-on-one informal meeting to help someone improve or make changes in behavior.

• **Performance review.** This is a more structured review of competencies or behaviors with specific ratings to identify problem areas.

• **Written reprimand.** This document details specifically what's wrong, what needs to change, and what will happen if changes aren't made. All written warnings should be reviewed in a meeting with the person involved.

• **Formal warning.** In this conversation it's best to include an additional leader who can address the problem and affirm the authority of the supervisor. Typically this conversation includes a warning that failure to make improvements or comply may result in termination.

• **Time off.** For staff members, this may take the form of a paid or unpaid suspension. Volunteers may need to be temporarily removed from their ministry roles.

• **Termination.** For staff this includes ending the employment. It may also include removing the person from your fellowship.

One key to successfully using this continuum of care is to make sure there are no surprises. For example, it should not be a surprise to a staff member if one day you are sitting with him or her and discussing termination of employment. These people should know ahead of time that the magnitude of their actions justifies termination, or they should have received adequate warnings along the way so the action does not come as a surprise.

Second, the consequences should match the offense. It's acceptable to skip steps along the continuum based on the actions of the employee or volunteer. Criminal acts and significant moral failures, for example, must be handled swiftly and decisively.

Communicate clearly. Document everything. Be consistent. Be decisive. Don't procrastinate. Fortunately, most situations can be handled simply through coaching. You need to be prepared, however, to handle tough situations head-on.

—Tony

Partner for the Long Term

I may be the biggest bargain hunter alive today. At least, I used to be. When I shopped, I would literally spend months researching the item. By the time I chose the item, I knew more about it than the engineers who designed it. Then, when I knew which item I would purchase, I would scour the Internet, looking for the best price. It didn't matter where I'd purchased similar items in the past. I knew what I wanted, and I would buy it from whoever gave me the lowest price.

I'm changing. I'm beginning to realize the value of trust, integrity, and a solid reputation. I'm learning about the value of developing long-term relationships with vendors in whom I have confidence—people I know will stand behind their products.

If this is true when buying a $200 camera, then it applies when spending thousands of dollars on a product or millions of dollars on a church building. My advice is to look for vendors, contractors, and architects with whom you can develop long-term partnerships. Then work hard to develop those relationships.

Here are some advantages of long-term partnerships:

• **You won't need to re-educate your partners each time.** There are so many values that make your church unique. Long-term partners begin to recite your mission and values before you do.

• **You save time** during each project's research and interview process.

• **You develop trust** in each other. You don't have to wonder about their honesty. You've seen it demonstrated over time.

• **You have opportunities for life-changing ministry** with the vendors. Many times, it's necessary to invest years in a relationship before you're able to win someone's trust in order to effectively share your faith.

• **The quality of the craftsmanship and service is improved.** Why? Because they expect and want your future business. It's not just about this project or purchase. It's about keeping you a happy client for years to come.

• **The blame game is minimized.** You don't hear statements such as

"The last contractor really messed this up. It's going to cost more money to fix it," or "When we gave our quote, we weren't aware of..." Since they've been involved all along, there are fewer surprises and no one else to blame.

Save yourself time, money, and headaches by partnering for the long term.

—Tim

75 Teach the Tithe Regularly

"On every Lord's Day, each of you should put aside some amount of money in relation to what you have earned and save it for this offering" (1 Corinthians 16:2, NLT).

Maybe this isn't true in your church, but ours is filled with people who did not grow up in the church. Because of that, they aren't familiar with how the church works. That gives us freedom to communicate the gospel of Jesus Christ without having to explain traditions that may be difficult to understand in today's culture. One of the challenges associated with having lots of people who are unchurched, however, is that they aren't accustomed to *giving* their money to anyone, particularly a church. Around our church, we celebrate when giving doesn't seem to be keeping pace with attendance growth because it typically means we're reaching our target—people who haven't yet met Jesus.

In fact, we even go a step further in our services. We tell people *not* to give. We frequently communicate it from the platform, and it's printed in the bulletin every week. Here's what we say: "Bringing a gift to God is a regular part of our worship. If you're a guest today, we want you to know that you are under no obligation to give. This service is our gift to you."

> Giving *is* an act of worship.

That's what we tell visitors. At the same time, however, we don't shrink from teaching about biblical stewardship. Giving is an act of worship. As people meet Jesus and begin to take steps in their faith journeys, we don't hold back from sharing what Scriptures say about giving. We talk about the Old Testament laws about tithing, and we teach about the New Testament principles of sacrificial giving in response to our relationship with Jesus. We teach it to our believers at the midweek service. We teach it to our members through the classes we offer. At least twice a year, we even teach it to the weekend crowd with "seekers" present. The point is, people will not learn to put God first with the resources he has provided until they learn the concept of stewardship—of their life and their resources—taught in the Bible.

In his book, *How to Increase Giving in Your Church*, George Barna writes, "Churches in which pastors preach a series of messages about giving are nearly two-and-a-half times more likely to experience an increase in giving than when preachers speak about giving, one sermon at a time, on two or more nonconsecutive occasions during the year."

Include personal testimonies when you talk about money.

We've experienced this at Granger. The real impact of teaching on giving occurs when we hit the topic two or more weeks in a row. (Just this year, our offerings jumped 34 percent after a four-week tithe series.)

Here's one hint: Include personal testimonies when you talk about money. The messages that God communicates through "regular people" are frequently much more powerful than those the paid preacher delivers. But don't hold back. Teach the truth about giving confidently and regularly.

—Tony

76 Throw a Party for the Smallest Success

Our youngest child, Taylor, just turned two years old. In our family, we are trying to develop a culture of cheering the smallest victories in his life. His three older siblings are also enjoying it. When he throws a piece of paper in the trash, we cheer. When he puts his toys back in the toy box, we cheer. Often our older children will call from a distance, "Come, everyone, see what Taylor is doing!" We all rush, watch the way he's stacked the blocks or colored the monkey, and we all clap and cheer, saying, "Yea, Taylor!" He grins hugely, and we can see beneath the smile a sense of acceptance and achievement.

We are all two-year-olds at heart, aren't we? We love to be cheered. We love to be affirmed. We like to be noticed for the little things we do. Even though our heart's desire is to deflect the attention to God, it feels good to be appreciated.

However, when we grow up, we tend to overanalyze potential responses to our praise. We might think, "If I praise him too early, he may think the job is done and he doesn't have to finish." Or "If I give her too much praise for a small success, what am I going to do for something big?" Or "If I make a big deal about this, won't that set a precedent, forcing me to do the same thing every time for everyone?"

Let me encourage you with this advice: Just do it. Don't think about it. Don't determine your action based on a predicted response. Just do it. Don't worry about precedent or patterns or "what ifs." Just choose to develop a culture in your life, and in your congregation, in which the smallest successes are noticed and affirmed.

Here are a few ways that we've "thrown parties" for small successes at Granger:

• **Silly gifts.** Find opportunities to say thanks to people in unique ways. We've given Rescue Heroes to a small-group leader in the children's department for doing her part to help rescue kids. We gave a baseball bat to the leader who continually "hits the ball out of the park." Be creative. Give a traffic cone signed by all the pastors to the guy who faithfully helps people find a place to park.

• **Sermons.** When you deliver a message on serving, use several illustrations of people in the church who serve faithfully behind the scenes. Talk about the lady who washes all the nursery toys every Monday morning, or the team that records and duplicates all the message tapes, or the volunteers who prune the trees and weed the flower beds.

• **Group recognition.** Ask all those who are greeters to stand during your service, and let everyone cheer for them. Or show a video of the joyful interaction between nursery workers and the kids in their care, and after the video cheer the workers' faithful service.

There is really no way to mess this up—just do it. Model this attitude for your church, and develop a "partylike" culture in which people are always being cheered and affirmed for their contributions to the mission. Start today.

—Tim

Affinity and Diversity Can Walk Hand in Hand

"Some of us are Jews, some are Gentiles, some are slaves, and some are free. But we have all been baptized into Christ's body by one Spirit, and we have all received the same Spirit" (1 Corinthians 12:13, NLT).

At Granger, we do everything together. We meet together. We eat together. We play together. We pray together. We attend conferences together.

A couple of years ago we purchased our first shuttle buses to help move people from the parking lots to our building entrance and to provide transportation for road trips. When we ordered the buses, we opted not to have the seats line up in rows through the length of the bus. Instead, the seats were configured in a circle so that everyone can see everyone else's face. It creates conversation and fellowship. So now when we travel, we even travel in community.

Now you're probably saying to yourself, "Doing everything as a team is great as long as you like everyone else." Well, that's the case on our team. And I think one of the key reasons is the fact that we pay attention to affinity when we're adding someone to our team. When we hire new people or select someone for a lay leadership role, we're not only looking for Christ followers who can perform a particular function. We're also looking for people with whom we want to share life. We want fun people. We want people who are creative and innovative. We're looking for positive types, people who love to encourage and draw the best out of others. We're looking for people who are more inclined to show grace than to condemn.

The important thing to remember, however, is that affinity and diversity *can* walk hand in hand. Our staff and lay leadership team is composed of people of many cultural and economic backgrounds. We have men *and women* in key leadership roles. Just as diversity strengthens a team, affinity creates a bond that's not easily broken.

—Tony

78 Send Lots of Handwritten Notes

When I was in ninth grade, Miss Wessel took our student council team on a retreat. For two days, about thirty students from our school spent time together learning, growing, and getting to know each other. I'll never forget one exercise. At the beginning of the retreat, she gave us each a paper lunch sack and some crayons and asked us to draw a picture on the sack. It seemed a little juvenile for a bunch of cool junior high kids. But because we liked Miss Wessel, we went with it.

Then we wrote our names on our "artwork" and lined up our colorful lunch sacks on a table. Miss Wessel then gave us this assignment: "Sometime in the next two days, write a note to put in each bag that tells that person what you appreciate or respect about him or her."

That was over twenty-five years ago, and I still have the notes that were addressed to me. Occasionally I take them out and read these notes from thirty of my peers who said nice things about my personality, my leadership, and my contribution to the school. The experience put wind in my sails. It filled my emotional tank. It gave me confidence and strength. And it permanently engraved in my mind the importance of written notes of appreciation.

When I first came to Granger, I was reintroduced to this type of culture. "Send Three Postcards Each Week" was the standard. We all did it. We provided postcards for volunteer leaders and encouraged them to do the same. We said, "Find people doing things right and let them know you appreciate it." Or "Encourage three people you saw serving on Sunday, and send them each a postcard." Or "Look for people serving behind the scenes, and tell them how grateful you are for their faithfulness." I once visited the house of one of our members and saw posted on the refrigerator a card I had mailed three years earlier.

Words of appreciation are powerful. They can be life-changing. It takes just a few minutes to write on a postcard, but the impact will last for weeks or months. It costs about a quarter, but the investment will be returned again and again. Make it a habit. Make it part of your culture.

—Tim

Reward the Person Who Stops a Dead Program

In addition to acknowledging leaders who effectively expand ministry, make sure you appropriately celebrate the leader who ends a program that is ineffective or not aligned with your church's mission or strategy. Don't get caught in the "we've always done it this way" trap. Instead, encourage people to ask whether or not it's best to continue a particular ministry program.

Here is a list of ministry ideas and programs we've ended at Granger:

• Gen-X weekend services
• intensive Bible studies for students as primary outreach
• building committees
• 8:00 a.m. Sunday services
• classes as primary adult-discipleship programs
• twelve-week membership classes

Of these programs or ideas, some had minimal initial success, but all of them ended up having little impact. That's not to suggest that they won't work in your ministry environment, because we've seen successful examples of each.

We supported the Gen-X service, for example, with a full two years of staffing, financial resources, promotions, and volunteer effort. By the end of those two years, attendance was actually lower than when the program was first started. There are probably a number of reasons it wasn't as successful as we had hoped. The primary reason was that our "regular" weekend services were already targeting a much younger audience than most churches (our average adult attendee is thirty-five years old). Rather than continuing to pour time and resources into trying to make the Gen-X service grow, we elected to end it. That allowed us to focus energies on our other weekend services and free up staff and volunteers to pursue other ministry opportunities. As with all major changes, ending this effort required communication, time, and prayer, but doing so has definitely paid dividends for our church in the long run.

> Create a culture in which change is not only tolerated, it's expected.

One side benefit of rewarding people who stop dead programs is that it encourages people to take risks. Your team will soon learn that it's OK to try out a new approach to see if it will be successful. If it doesn't work, you can just stop doing it. This helps create a culture in which change is not only tolerated, it's expected. People will get very creative if they know you're going to reward their attempts to bring about positive change, whether that change is successful or not.

—Tony

80 Don't Let Your Board Decide How Many Pencils to Purchase

Many times we believe we are valuing the time of our people by letting them make decisions. Sometimes that is true. But when members of our board are making decisions that are not critical to our mission, we are *wasting* their time, not *valuing* it.

It's not that they won't have opinions. It's not that their opinions aren't valuable. It's just not a good use of their time.

A few years ago at Granger, we realized we were spending a lot of time getting our lay board up to speed so they could make the same decisions we would have made without them. This may also be true in your church if you have lay board members. They spend fifty-plus hours per week at a job, then come to the church office for evening meetings. They are tired and would love to be spending time with their families. We think we're doing them a favor by involving them in decision making. They want to be helpful, so they give their time to what we think is important. But it takes many hours to give them enough information to make an informed decision—hours they could have spent in meaningful ministry.

I've learned that anytime you ask people to express an opinion, they'll have one. However, just because they have an opinion about something doesn't mean their feelings will be hurt if you don't ask. And it doesn't mean that it's a good use of their time to ask them.

I propose a very different way to look at your church board. Value their time by asking them to spend time in what they do best. Ask for their "fresh eyes" on church services and ministry events. Have them help evaluate ministry effectiveness filtered through the mission, vision, and values of the church.

I've heard Rick Warren say many times, "The people are the ministers; the staff are the *ad*-ministers." If your church is two hundred or larger in size, then it is too big for lay volunteers to be involved in its daily operational decisions.

—Tim

81 Spouses Should Share the Experience

"And the Lord God said, 'It is not good for the man to be alone. I will make a companion who will help him'" (Genesis 2:18, NLT).

I've worked in several organizations outside of ministry that allowed my work life to be my work life and my family life to be my family life. In ministry, however, I just don't believe that model coincides with God's plan for marriage. Ministry needs to be a partnership within the framework of the marriage covenant. Some spouses may choose to be more involved than others. Not every marriage will be like Priscilla and Aquila's; they were co-workers in ministry. The fact is, however, the line between ministry life and family life is blurry.

> Ministry needs to be a partnership within the framework of the marriage covenant.

You should set up boundaries to protect the quality of your time with your spouse and your children, but I don't think that boundary will ever be a solid line. Allow for the ebb and flow of ministry and family life. Sometimes ministry will require demanding hours and most of your energy. Other times, you'll need to take time out from your church to give your family undivided attention and care. The point is, though, we teach our people that they *are* the ministers of the gospel. Their ministry takes place primarily outside the walls of the church building. The same holds true for those of us who also happen to get a paycheck for our roles in the church. There's not a clean break. I'm not advocating eighty-hour workweeks. I'm just saying you shouldn't feel guilty when ministry crosses over from time to time into the family arena.

Likewise, I think we need to find ways for families, especially spouses, to participate in the ministry experience. I'm especially concerned about learning experiences—at times one person in the marriage relationship is off participating in extensive biblical teaching or ministry training or enjoying a phenomenal worship experience. As that person learns, he or she is also growing apart from his or her spouse if the two aren't sharing the time. I've heard others say, "Education is alienation." It's true. It's difficult to completely communicate a training or conference experience to someone who hasn't participated in it firsthand.

When you send your staff members to training, offer opportunities for their spouses to join them if possible. When you don't, you're encouraging one person in the relationship to take steps in ministry and in his or her spiritual journey that the other is missing.

—Tony

82 Answer the Phone

A couple of years ago, the Barna Research Group conducted a study to determine the general accessibility of church representatives to people who contacted the church by telephone. The results indicated that personal contact was never established in 40 percent of the churches called, in spite of multiple callbacks. Of those churches in which no one answered, almost half didn't even have an answering machine to record messages. What an indictment of the church's ability to respond to the needs of our communities!

We need to make it as easy as possible for people to connect with our churches. Even if you're unable to hire someone or recruit volunteers to answer phones, very affordable technologies are available that provide voice mail or call-forwarding services so no call goes unanswered.

This may sound simple, but you should get in the habit of periodically trying to call your church to see how your systems are working. How long does it take for someone to pick up the phone? Are you placed on hold? Does the voice mail system operate properly? Are you ever inadvertently cut off? These first impressions communicate a lot. If people have initial encounters filled with frustration because they can't successfully maneuver through your phone system, they'll quickly assume your church isn't capable of helping them.

Once you receive the calls, you must also be prepared to respond.

Do you have systems in place for emergency care and counseling? Who's responsible for hospital visitation? If people leave voice mail messages, does someone respond promptly?

It's your responsibility to make sure the systems are in place, but you don't have to be the "super pastor" who personally handles every call to action. At Granger, for example, our voice mail system is set up to automatically page our volunteer leader to handle hospital-visitation requests. She receives the page and notifies someone from her team to make the visit. In certain situations, she's also been trained to contact a pastor for assistance. There's no need for the pastor to always be "the" person on call. There are people in your church who would love the opportunity to care for others. This is one more way that you can help equip the church to be the church.

—Tony

83 Eliminate the Committees and Multiply the Ministry

I once attended a church that had so many committees it even had a "Committee of Committees" to keep all the other committees organized. That's too many committees.

Consider these differences between a committee and a team:

A committee...	A team...
• decides.	• does.
• is boring.	• is exciting.
• exists to set policy.	• exists to win.
• will *drain* the life out of you.	• will *add* life to you.
• is for those who desire status.	• is for those who want to make a difference.

At Granger, we decided several years ago that we wanted people in ministry, not meetings. So we don't have any committees. None. Nada. Zero. Zilch.

We are a staff-led church with a lay-led board of directors. The board meets eight times each year. Its job is to champion the mission, vision, and values of the church. Its job is to make sure we are balancing the five purposes of the church. Other than that, we don't have a building committee; we don't have trustees; we don't have a personnel committee or finance committee or women's committee or youth committee. Any group that gets together at Granger is a ministry team, and each team does ministry. Of course, every ministry team's members meet occasionally to plan, reflect, set goals, and measure performance, but their primary function is ministry.

Perhaps your church is set up the same way, but the only difference is that you use the word *committee* instead of *team*. Let me encourage you to change your terminology. The word *team* connotes vision, goals, purpose, unity, equal effort, and accomplishment. On the other hand, the word *committee* just sucks the life right out of you. It communicates bureaucracy, policy, power, status, and lots of meetings. Doesn't it make you tired just thinking about it?

If your church's culture values people more highly in meetings than in ministry, then you need to begin to change your culture. If your church has a team mind-set but uses the word *committee* instead of *team*, then you need to change your terminology and re-educate your congregation on the difference.

God calls us to ministry, not meetings. Eliminate the committees at your church and watch the ministry multiply.

—Tim

8 Surround Yourself With Learners

"The wise accumulate knowledge—a true treasure; know-it-alls talk too much—a sheer waste" (Proverbs 10:14, The Message).

When you're looking for people to add to your ministry team, one of the first things you should determine is whether the people you're considering are learners. These are the people who understand that life is a journey, that they'll never arrive. Since they are aware that they don't know it all, they are more apt to let God control their lives and their ministries than to insist on sitting in the driver's seat. Learners aren't satisfied with the way things have always been done. They know someone has already figured out a better approach.

Learners are readers. They spend their free time roaming the aisles of bookstores. Learners are listeners. They want to know what makes others tick. Learners ask questions. They're not afraid to reveal their ignorance in order to obtain understanding.

The best learners are well-rounded in their pursuit of knowledge and understanding. You should try to find people for your team who are committed to being students in four areas.

Students of Scripture. Diving into God's Word gives us the foundation for how we do everything in life, including how we most effectively fulfill our ministry roles. The Bible says that's really all we need. "As we know Jesus better, his divine power gives us everything we need for living a godly life. He has called us to receive his own glory and goodness!" (2 Peter 1:3 NLT). Learners always begin with God's Word.

Students of leadership. Today there's really no excuse for not knowing basic leadership skills. Opportunities abound to learn leadership principles through books, magazines, conferences, and tapes. Pastors, in particular, need to be students of leadership. It's not enough to teach and shepherd. Whether you are a senior pastor or a small-group leader, you need to be a student of leadership. Others are counting on you to cast a compelling vision, successfully implement a

strategic plan, and demonstrate leadership skills that best use the servants
and resources God has provided.

Students of culture. If there's anything our experience has taught us at
Granger, it's that people crave spiritual
truth when it's presented in a culturally
relevant context. We've used movies, television, and current events to teach peo-

> People crave spiritual truth when it's presented in a culturally relevant context.

ple about the hope and unconditional love found only in Jesus Christ.
To minister effectively in today's culture, you need to be a student of
that culture. Paul demonstrated it best when he approached ministry
differently with the Jews than he did with the Gentiles (see 1 Corinthians 9:19-23).

Students of successful ministries. Somebody's already done it.
Somewhere there is a church that's already dealt with the issues
you're facing. Learn from their successes and their failures. Whether
you're interested in creative arts, campus development, or ministry
strategy, take the time to find out what's working in other churches.
If it works in one location, it very well might work in your community.

—Tony

85 You Can't Overcommunicate the Vision

Have you heard any of these statements?

"Vision leaks."

"You must recast the vision every twenty-seven days."

"Without vision, the people perish."

Every church has to define its unique DNA when it is fairly young (or going through a transition) and then be ready to communicate that vision again and again and again.

You might ask, "What is the difference between a vision statement and a mission statement? Are we talking about communication of our vision? our purpose? our mission? our goals? When you say, 'Communicate the vision,' just what exactly are you talking about?"

The answer is *all of it.* In general, when we say that vision leaks if it is not constantly recommunicated, we are talking about the total package that defines your church. At Granger, our vision, or unique DNA, includes the following facets:

Our purposes. These communicate why every church exists.

Our mission statement. This communicates specifically why our church exists.

Our vision statement. This paints a picture of how our church will look in ten years.

Our values. This states how we'll live together as we accomplish our mission.

Our statement of faith. This communicates the doctrinal essentials that hold us together.

Our goals. These are written annually to focus our energy on certain areas.

This vision is not just a set of written documents. It must be taught, preached, written, and communicated in as many creative ways as possible. There is no "Communicate this until..." There is no "until." It will never be done. You will always have new people who have never heard it and "seasoned" people who have forgotten.

Here are some ways to communicate the vision:

• Deliver a weekend series every year that recasts the vision for your church. Then market the tapes or CDs of those messages for those who came to the church after the series concluded.

• Use your church newsletter or e-mail updates to consistently share the vision.

• Use stories to illustrate the impact of the vision.

• Teach it in your membership class.

• Provide small-group or Sunday-school curriculum that gives your veteran members a chance to study it again.

• Print your mission statement on every weekend program or bulletin.

• Use architecture to emphasize various statements. You can etch your vision in glass, imprint it on signage, or carve it in concrete.

• In smaller meetings, use fun memory games (and prizes!) to encourage people to continually review the vision.

Even pastors sometimes forget the vision. Figure out a personal system that will regularly remind you of why you are leading the church.

Remember, without vision, the people perish.

—Tim

86 Build Budgets on Purpose

At Granger, we've tried to build budgets based on the five purposes of the church and not based on last year's budget. This means we're focusing on what we should do next to connect people to fellowship, spiritual maturity, ministry service, missions, and worship. We try to take a fresh look each year so we're not continuing programs and practices just because we've always had them.

Instead of making across-the-board percentage adjustments to the previous year's budget, we've tried to develop our budgets based on an action plan. That plan is centered on helping us fulfill our mission and vision. That means there have been instances when some ministry areas saw significant budget increases while others experienced budget freezes or reductions.

Begin your budget process by defining your ministry plan. Each ministry area should develop a list of specific goals for the coming year. Then these questions should be asked about each goal:

- What are we trying to accomplish?
- What action steps will we take to reach this goal?
- How will this goal help us accomplish our mission and vision?
- Who will lead? Who will help?
- What resources are needed?
- What is our target date for completion?

Your primary goal is to fulfill biblical purposes rather than to maintain fairness and equality.

These questions drive the budgeting for each area. They force leaders to consider proactive steps for accomplishing the vision rather than just *maintaining* current ministry efforts. Where there is no vision, the budgets perish.

After you've determined how much money is available, budget based on what you'll need to enact the action plan your leadership team has developed for the coming year. Be sure that your primary goal is to fulfill biblical purposes rather than to maintain fairness and equality.

While you're doing this, remember that the treasurer shouldn't set the budget. He or she should simply facilitate the budgeting process. At Granger, we encourage ministry leaders to develop their budget proposals as teams. After the budgets are submitted, the senior and executive pastors determine final budget targets for each ministry area and ask the area leaders to either increase or decrease their budget proposals based on the overall direction of the church. Once the budget is balanced, the senior management team makes the final recommendation to the administrative board, which has the final authority to approve the annual budget.

The process should be structured to maintain accountability with the resources God has provided for your ministry, but accountability begins with identifying the purpose for every dollar you plan to spend.

—Tony

87 E-Mail Can Get You in Trouble

I just checked. I've received 11,884 e-mails in the past year at the church. E-mail can be a very efficient means of communication. It helps me multitask. It helps me maintain contact with people I might otherwise never talk to. It helps me organize my communication.

Despite these benefits, e-mail can get us into trouble. Again and again I've seen miscommunication, relational explosions, and deeply hurt people as a result of e-mail. Here are some of the advantages *and* disadvantages of e-mail.

The Good	The Bad
• Can be copied easily to many people.	• Can be copied easily to many people.
• For those who are orally challenged, it can be an easier way to express thoughts.	• You can't read their eyes.
• Quick. Saves time.	• You can't see their hearts.
• Can include Web links or attached documents.	• You can't tell what's being understood or what needs further explanation.

Most of the time, e-mail is a very appropriate way to communicate. However, there are certain times when you should avoid e-mail:
- When you are in any type of relational conflict with an individual.
- When you are mad.
- When you don't trust someone, or you think he or she doesn't trust you.
- When you are hurt by something someone just wrote to you.
- When you are writing anything that would not be OK if seen by everyone in your church.

• When your heart is beating hard, your fingers are typing fast, and you know you'll feel vindicated when you finally hit the "send" button.

Whenever there is any degree of tension in your relationship with another individual, don't communicate by e-mail. Talk with him or her in person so that you can see the eyes, watch the body language, and sense the person's spirit. If the individual is too far away to talk with in person, then pick up the phone and call him or her. That way, you can distinguish voice inflections and detect the emotion behind the words.

There are some people you should never e-mail. The dynamics between you may require that you always communicate in person. You'll want to do whatever is necessary to keep these relationships healthy. So think before you hit "send."

—Tim

88 Give Volunteers an Experience, Not Just a Task

"Think of ways to encourage one another to outbursts of love and good deeds" (Hebrews 10:24, NLT).

I've worked in ministry and in the marketplace, and I can tell you it's much easier leading in the marketplace. Out in the business world, people do what you ask them to do because they're paid to do it. Ministry, however, is the true measure of leadership because people are giving their time and talents because they *want* to serve. Ultimately, they serve because they've been called by God to fulfill a specific mission. Whether they're singing a solo or stuffing bulletins, these servants understand that their contributions are helping people take their next steps toward Christ.

One of the primary roles of a ministry leader is to remind people why they're serving. People will get burned out on ministries that involve only completing a task. On the other hand, they'll give their lives to a ministry task performed with others, to fulfill a greater mission. Good leaders are skilled at training and equipping people to do a specific job. The best leaders also know how to draw the best out of people and help them commit for the long haul.

To draw the best out of your volunteer teams, you must care for them. Find out what's happening in their lives. Take time to learn about their families, their jobs, and their walks with Christ. Share celebrations and disappointments. Pray for them. Pray together.

Take time to honor them for their service. Tell them individually how their contributions are having an eternal impact. Send lots of handwritten notes. Encourage them to take additional steps and make new commitments. In front of others, acknowledge their roles in the ministry. And periodically give them gifts to show your appreciation for their service. The gift might be as simple as sharing a meal to mark the completion of a critical ministry run.

You can also move beyond just completing the task by creating opportunities for people to build relationships with others. Team people up in roles that are typically accomplished by one person. It will be those relationships that keep people coming back over time. We have a group of women in our church who regularly gather to help prepare bulk mailings. They aren't compelled to get together because of the thousands of labels they get to stick on envelopes. Rather, what they won't give up is the devotional time and conversation they share when they gather.

It's all about serving Jesus, but it's more fun to do that in an environment in which people care about and encourage one another. That's when ministry moves from being a task to being an experience.

—Tony

89 Leave Well

Have you ever noticed that when some people decide to leave your church they often vomit on their way out? No, it's not last night's supper. Rather, what comes out are all their gripes and complaints about you and the church. This has happened many times at Granger. Sometimes I want to shake them and say, "If you don't like it, just leave quietly! Bless another church with your rotten attitude, but don't spew all your complaints over everyone around you on your way out."

Awhile back, we released a pastor from his ministry. Because of that decision, about sixty families left the church. It was amazing how mean-spirited many of them were as they left. Many of them had found Christ at Granger, and all of them had grown in their faith, but most didn't say thanks for any of that. They just talked about their anger and the stupidity of the leaders who made the decision.

> When some staff members resign their positions, they feel a need to justify their departure by bad-mouthing the church they are leaving.

There was one family, though, that left well. Mike and Laura left with dignity and integrity. They wrote a letter and, rather than sheepishly mailing it, they came by the office to read it aloud to us. They thanked the church for the wonderful ministry their family had received over the years. They honored the pastor for his role in their spiritual development. They said they did not agree with the recent decision, but they did not slander anyone or make mean comments. They left the church, but we never heard any report of their gossiping or griping to others. They left well.

This should also be true of pastors and staff members. For some reason, when some staff members resign their positions, they feel a need to justify their departure by bad-mouthing the church they are leaving. Or they wait until they leave town and then talk negatively by phone and e-mail with people still in the church. This dishonors Christ and our Christian brothers and sisters.

Important Rules for Leaving

Before You Resign (while making your decision)

• Don't discuss with anyone in the church or on staff your complaints about the church or its leaders. If you need counsel, get it from someone out of town.

After You Resign

• Don't talk negatively to anyone.

• People will come to you with their gripes and complaints because they want the inside scoop. Resist. Be blunt with them. Tell them that you will not enter into such conversations.

• Talk freely about everything you'll miss at the church. Talk about the things you love, the stuff you've learned, and the way you've grown.

After You Are Gone

• Don't listen to gripes or complaints from people about the church you left. Never. None. No exceptions.

• Honor and respect your replacement.

• Don't go back to the church for at least one year. Give the church time to grow and move on without you. This will allow no opportunity for comparisons.

Remember that there is more at stake than your own reputation. It is the reputation of Christ in the church and the community that should be your concern. So, for God's sake, leave well.

—Tim

90 Numbers Communicate Momentum, and Momentum Generates Numbers

Have you heard any of these statements?

"At our church, we don't care about numbers...we care about people."

"Our church doesn't count attendance because we don't want to get caught up in comparisons with other churches."

"A lot of churches are fourteen miles wide and only three inches deep," which means they attract a lot of people but don't have much depth.

Those types of statements preach well and may draw a lot of "amens" from the crowd, but what do they communicate? Do they communicate that what we are doing in the church isn't important enough to measure? Do they communicate that we don't want to know if we are losing people?

> **We count people because people count.**

Counting is biblical, you know. There happens to be a whole book in the Old Testament filled with numbers. In fact, it's even called Numbers. Someone counted the disciples of Jesus. There were twelve. On the day of Pentecost someone counted and recorded the three thousand that were added to the church. The Bible is filled with numbers!

People matter to God. We count people because people count. Whatever your mission, whatever your vision as a church, you have to count. There are many different ways to determine whether you are accomplishing your mission and completing your vision. Measure. Record. Compare.

It's not just Sunday morning attendance that you should measure. How many are connected in small groups? How many attend Sunday school? How many have been baptized? How many are serving in ministry? How many are leaders? How many are giving an offering regularly? How many are tithing? How many are gathering for worship? How many are involved in outreach or missions? How do these numbers compare to last year's? Are we growing? Are we losing ground in any area?

Once you have the numbers, creatively communicate them to your congregation in order to motivate, inspire, challenge, or generate involvement.

Here are some motivational ways we have used numbers in recent months:

• "Many of you gave sacrificially to finish the Children's Center. I want you to know that fifty-six children gave their lives to Christ last weekend."

• "Many of you are inviting your friends to church. This month we are averaging fifteen hundred more people in attendance than we were this same month last year. Way to go, church!"

• "Our attendance has increased 40 percent since last year, and yet our number of leaders has only increased 5 percent. This may be the time for some of you to say, 'Count me in. I'll give my leadership gifts to Jesus!' "

• "We have three children for every one adult each weekend in our services...Wow, you are a prolific group!"

Numbers, when communicated clearly, will generate the momentum your church may need to accomplish its mission. Each number represents a life that Christ died for. Numbers (people) matter to God, and they should matter to you.

—Tim

Your New Staff Member Already Attends Your Church

I recently analyzed fifteen years of hiring history at Granger. I categorized every person ever on staff as a "successful" staff hire or an "unsuccessful" staff hire. I considered the hire successful either if the person is still on staff or if he or she left well without conflict. If he or she was fired or resigned and left with difficulty, then I considered that an unsuccessful staff hire. The results were amazing! Of those we hired from outside the church, 50 percent were successful hires, and 50 percent weren't. But when I looked at those we've hired from within the church, 95 percent were successful, and only 5 percent weren't. I've heard similar findings again and again from other church leaders.

Here's why hiring from inside makes so much sense:

• These people *know* the mission, vision, and values. There won't be any surprises six months after they join the staff.

• They *love* the mission, vision, and values. It's not just head knowledge—their lives have been changed as a result of the church's ministry.

• You know how well they are *respected* by the other volunteers or staff. You wouldn't be interviewing them if you didn't know they're respected.

Chemistry matters. It helps enormously if you like the people on your team.

• You know whether you like them. The importance of *chemistry* on your team cannot be overemphasized. Bill Hybels once said in a conference, "Do you know how to determine if you've hired the right person? When you're working in your office and they stick their head in the door and say, 'Do you have a minute?' and at that moment, you're happy inside—then you hired the right person." His point: Chemistry matters. It helps enormously if you like the people on your team.

- You know how they *respond* under pressure. You've seen them in some tough times and in some awkward situations. You don't have to wonder how they'll respond the first time they're backed into a corner.

- You know in what ways they're really *strong*. They have strengths you need, and you've seen these strengths in action.

- You know their *weaknesses*. Everyone has weaknesses. When you hire from inside, you already know most of the weaknesses of the person you are hiring.

It's natural to quickly look over one's congregation and think, "No one here has the qualifications we need." Look again. "We need someone with experience." Look again. "We want someone who has been further down the road than we are." Look again.

Most churches consider these traits to be vitally important when hiring:

- **Skills.** Are they trained in the specific task?
- **Experience.** Have they been successful doing it somewhere else?
- **Leadership.** Can they grow in their capacity and responsibilities?
- **Ability.** Can they get the job done?
- **Passion.** Does it make their hearts beat fast?
- **Heart.** Do they love the church and wholeheartedly believe in its mission, vision, and values?
- **Integrity.** Can I trust them?

That's a pretty good list. Most church leaders place the greatest emphasis on skills and experiences, and it is those two traits that fill most résumés. However, I believe they are the least important! If someone in your church isn't trained and doesn't have experience in the role but has the other five traits, then hire that person! You can train him or her in a skill, and you can provide the necessary experience. But you can't train leadership capacity or the ability to complete the job—people either have these qualities or they don't. You also cannot quickly change a person's character. And it will take a lot of time before a newcomer to your church fully understands and loves its mission, vision, and values.

The next time you are recruiting for a new staff position, take a look inside your church first. You might save yourself a lot of heartache.

—Tim

92 Put Your Money Where Your Crowd Is

Here's a fun exercise to do with your leadership team. Have them turn to the Gospel of Mark, then ask them to identify the common theme in each of these verses concerning Jesus' ministry here on earth.

"Since they could not get him to Jesus because of the crowd, they made an opening in the roof above Jesus and, after digging through it, lowered the mat the paralyzed man was lying on" (Mark 2:4).

"Once again Jesus went out beside the lake. A large crowd came to him, and he began to teach them" (Mark 2:13).

"Jesus withdrew with his disciples to the lake, and a large crowd from Galilee followed. When they heard all he was doing, many people came to him from Judea, Jerusalem, Idumea, and the regions across the Jordan and around Tyre and Sidon. Because of the crowd he told his disciples to have a small boat ready for him, to keep the people from crowding him" (Mark 3:7-9).

> Churches that effectively communicate the gospel in today's culture will always attract crowds.

"Then Jesus entered a house, and again a crowd gathered, so that he and his disciples were not even able to eat" (Mark 3:20).

"Again Jesus began to teach by the lake. The crowd that gathered around him was so large that he got into a boat and sat in it out on the lake, while all the people were along the shore at the water's edge" (Mark 4:1).

Do you get the picture? These are only a few references. The list could go on. The point is this: Large crowds gathered wherever Jesus went. In recent years some have argued that megachurches may soon become a thing of the past. They suggest larger churches won't effectively reach postmoderns and their need for authentic relationships in smaller communities. I think churches that effectively communicate the gospel in today's culture will always attract crowds. People want to be a part of something that transforms lives.

In one of the passages cited above, Jesus was teaching beside a lake, and a large crowd gathered. As he was teaching, he noticed Levi, the tax collector. He called Levi out of the crowd, saying, "Follow me." We approach ministry at Granger the same way. We design services, programs, and events to draw a crowd, and then we create specific strategies to encourage people to follow Jesus. That's a distinction from other ministries that focus on building up the believers before trying to reach the crowd.

Without a crowd, there won't be anyone to take steps toward spiritual maturity. In order for ministry to remain healthy and balanced, you'll need to spend a higher percentage of your budget on attracting the crowd. At Granger, we've chosen to invest huge resources in things like advertising, stage sets for weekend services, children's ministry, and "First Impressions." We want the experience on the weekends to be very attractive. We're intentional about our plan to generate a crowd. In fact, over 70 percent of our programming budget is used for attracting the crowd to weekend services.

A balanced ministry doesn't necessarily mean equal financial resources for every ministry program. You need to put your money where your crowd is.

—Tony

93 Share Critical Knowledge, Even When It Hurts

Every church will face tough times. They might be caused by financial difficulties, the death of a loved leader in the church, or a disappointing setback. Sometimes these difficulties should be shared with the congregation.

Earlier in this book we talked about a time we raised two million dollars for an auditorium and later realized we would never build it. We had spent months casting the vision for a huge dream. But we learned that the building as it was designed was going to cost too much money. Finally, we had to ask, "What should we tell the church?"

Whenever you face a tough issue, you could communicate to the church in several ways. One way is to deliver the "spin." Make it look like a victory, not a setback. Make it appear that it doesn't bother you and that it really isn't a problem at all. Show that you really are going to be able to do exactly what you had planned; it will just look different. Have you heard politicians do that after a huge defeat? I can recall many politicians delivering the spin after the 1984 presidential election when Ronald Reagan won in a landslide. It was almost laughable to hear politicians tell the country that the election wasn't as decisive as it seemed, that the country was still very divided.

Another option is to communicate exactly how you are feeling. The problem with this approach is that you might be depressed, hopeless, and even doubting God. If you share the depths of your depression, then you might send your congregation home looking for razor blades and bottles of pills.

A third option, and the one that we chose, is to find a balance between frank honesty and intentional leadership, between a pessimistic view of the past and a prescriptive plan for the future. Here are some steps to follow:

• **Pick the right crowd.** In our case, we talked to all the people who had financially pledged to the project because we believed they had the greatest interest in it. At the same time, we didn't want to communicate "internal" difficulties to our guests at the weekend service.

• **Be honest but not hopeless.** It's OK to say, "Things didn't turn out as we'd hoped." It's fine to say, "We are disappointed." But then follow up with, "But we know God has something better for us. We know God is still on the throne. We know he isn't surprised by this."

• **Be human.** It's OK to say, "I don't have all the answers." You don't have to know everything. You don't have to fix everything.

• **Allow people time to mourn the loss.** Loss is hard. Many times leaders process pain more quickly than others. That may cause us to be insensitive to those we lead who may need more time to work through the grieving process.

• **Get help.** There are church leaders outside of your community with more experience, wisdom, and ability than you have. Ask for their insight. Learn from them. Don't be a lone ranger.

If you haven't made a mistake yet, you will. If your church hasn't hit a bump or two to slow you down, it's just a matter of time before it does. Determine, during those times, to share critical knowledge with the right people, even when it hurts.

—Tim

94 Recruit Constantly

"He said to his disciples, 'The harvest is so great, but the workers are so few. So pray to the Lord who is in charge of the harvest; ask him to send out more workers for his fields.' " (Matthew 9:37-38, NLT).

OK, I know this will sound almost sacrilegious to some of you. I know you're out there. You're the purists. You believe that when it comes to asking people to step into ministry, there's an appropriate path one must take. You must wait until they've attended your church for at least twelve months. They have to be Christ followers with baptism certificates to prove it. You require them to take a spiritual gifts inventory, a Myers-Briggs test, and a Scholastic Aptitude Test. They must meet with a ministry counselor, an ordained pastor, and the church elders to confirm their calling to a particular role. And then, only after due process, may they be offered the opportunity to serve in ministry.

> Some people in your church will never get connected in relationships and may never take steps in their spiritual journeys unless someone asks them to jump right into a ministry team.

Now, here's reality. Some people in your church will go through the strategic steps you've established to help them plug into ministry. Others in your church will never get connected in relationships and may never take steps in their spiritual journeys unless someone asks them to jump right into a ministry team. It may be only through that experience that they build the necessary trust with team members to ask the tough faith questions and meet Jesus for the first time. That's one of the reasons we try to create "easy access ministry" for people in almost every area of our church. These are roles that allow even seekers to participate and ultimately develop relationships that help them take steps toward Christ.

I'm always on the lookout for new people to fill ministry roles on my team. I try to get them plugged into ministry and help them develop relationships in which they'll experience both mentorship in their roles and discipleship in their faith journeys. Some ministry roles need committed Christ followers. Some need skilled technicians. Others need servants who are available and willing to be trained.

Here's how this works:

• **Identify** a ministry role that needs to be filled and the skills and personality that will best fit the position.

• **Pray.** Ask God to help you identify the person he has in mind for the role.

• **Ask** others if they know people who might be interested in the role.

• **Promote** available ministry positions through bulletin and Power-Point ads, ministry fairs, and Web site posts.

• Regularly **review** the list of new members to learn their occupations and how their life experiences might fit in your ministry.

• **Encourage** other leaders in your ministry area to use this same approach.

As a ministry leader, one of your primary roles is to recruit continuously in order to build teams and help people plug into ministry. You'll never have enough volunteers, so this process can never stop.

—Tony

95 Avoid Creating a "Federation of Subministries"

A couple of years ago, I visited a church with over five thousand attendees each week. I attended a service and met with some of the staff. I spent a couple of days learning from their experiences. But I was perplexed when I left. I observed many things that bothered me. For example,

• some staff members went weeks without seeing others on staff.

• most had no idea what was happening in the church outside of their own departments.

• none of the staff members I talked to had an idea of the overall vision of the church or how they fit into it.

• I heard lots of envious comments about budget allocation, room usage, and staff hires.

In my opinion, this was not a church. It was what I've heard Bill Hybels call a federation of subministries. These were separate ministries coexisting in one location. Each had its own mission, vision, and goals, and none had anything to do with the overall vision of the church. The church even had a tape for newcomers containing a message from each pastor. It was like listening to a sales pitch from six different CEOs of separate companies. There was no cohesiveness, unity, shared purpose, or common mission.

This is not God's idea of a church. God's idea involves community, affinity, and togetherness. A church is a group of people gathered around a common purpose and a shared goal. It is believers who come together to accomplish the Great Commission and the Great Commandment in their neighborhood or city.

But it isn't easy to stay unified. It takes intentional focus and hard work. It means fighting against the status quo and sometimes choosing an uncomfortable path. It requires strategic thinking and constant monitoring. Here are some tips for staying unified:

• Maintain a common budget.

- Organize your budget according to the purposes of the church.
- Don't allow departmental fundraising.
- Frequently schedule events, meetings, and parties to allow the entire staff or leadership group to be together.
- Create opportunities for departments to share their goals and dreams with one another.
- Constantly tell stories of life change to keep everyone focused on the purpose.
- End ineffective ministries. Dismiss ineffective staff or leaders.
- Schedule rooms according to ministry priority, not on a "first come, first served" basis.
- Hire staff according to ministry priority and potential return, not on the desires of the loudest whiner.

It's very, very hard to keep a growing church unified and focused on the vision. However, it is even harder and more painful to revive a church that has drifted into a federation of subministries.

—Tim

Hire an Administrator Before You Hire a Youth Pastor

This title is really a bit of an exaggeration. But the truth is, many churches wait way too long to hire their first administrator.

If your church is averaging three to four hundred people in attendance each weekend, it may very well be time for you to take this step. Typically at this time a pastor begins to feel the strains stemming from a lack of systems and financial controls. This is also the time that churches often begin to consider stewardship campaigns and building expansions. At this point, leaders will begin to feel overwhelmed by the church's administrative demands. These are all signals that it's time to hire a church administrator.

As your church continues to grow, you may also want to consider splitting the responsibilities between an administrator and an executive pastor. We did this at Granger when we reached about twelve hundred in weekend attendance. Of course, these are the types of moves that not everyone is going to understand or support. Does it really take two people to handle the administration of a church? That's going to be tough for some people to grasp; however, addressing the infrastructure issues early will allow you to reach more people down the road.

At Granger, the administrative pastor handles all the day-to-day functions that support the frontline ministries of the church. These include insurance administration, finances, facility maintenance, office management, computer technology, Web site development, and human resource functions. The executive pastor focuses more on long-term projects, including strategic planning, stewardship campaigns, campus development, and staff leadership. This frees the senior pastor to champion the vision, address leadership development, and pour energy into preaching and teaching.

—Tony

Put This Word in Your Vocabulary: *Newness*

I've been in over a thousand church facilities. The overall appearance of 90 percent of them was dirty and unkempt, and they exhibited one or more of the following evidences of neglect:

- walls in need of painting
- water-stained ceiling tiles
- drywall in need of patching
- wallpaper that should be replaced
- pews or seat cushions in need of repair
- flower beds full of weeds
- yellowed or cracked fluorescent lighting
- worn carpet

Why is it that God's house is often unclean and broken down? Why is it that the place we come to worship the God of the universe has worn carpet and chipped paint? What is it that causes a church member to say, "It's OK...it's just the church"?

At Granger, we made the conscious decision before building our first facility to build only what we could maintain. Our cleaning and maintenance philosophy is simple: "Keep the building in *newness* condition." If it's broken, fix it today. If it's dirty, clean it today.

Why? Because we believe to our core that excellence honors God and inspires people. We so radically believe that people matter to God that we remove every distraction that might prevent them from clearly hearing how much he loves them. We realize the building is not just for us. It is for the thousands in our community who don't have a relationship with God. We know people are making value judgments every minute of every day. How we care for our grounds and facility makes a statement to the watching world about our faith and about our God.

Here are some suggestions for keeping your building in newness condition:

For those in an older building:

- Decide today to get your facility to newness condition.
- Through teaching and conversation, communicate to your congregation the value of caring for the house of God.

- Using volunteers or hired staff, take the weeks or months or years necessary to get your facility to a condition that's worthy of the God we serve.

- Once your facility has achieved newness condition, develop systems and assign staff or volunteers to keep it there.

For those building a new facility:

- Build only what you can care for with excellence.

- Determine your values for facility care before you start building.

Let's all do our part to take care of our churches. Let's develop a culture in which the congregation believes the value of excellence will help us reach more people for Christ. Let's all determine in our hearts to create houses of worship that will prompt the world to say, "Their God must matter!"

—Tim

98 Study Your Stats

"After a time of greeting and small talk, Paul told the story, detail by detail, of what God had done among the Gentiles through his ministry. They listened with delight and gave God the glory" (Acts 21:19-20, The Message).

I recently received an anonymous e-mail message from a believer who has never visited our church but happened to come across our Web site. This person sent one of those "I'm hurt, so I'm going to hurt you" messages trying to convince me that our ministry is misguided. In the message he wrote, "I am disturbed that you use numbers as an indication of success."

We are religious about very few things at Granger, but one thing we insist on is taking the pulse of our ministry. Each number reflects a changed life. Just read Acts, and you'll notice references throughout the book to the increasing number of people who became Christ followers and joined the early church. Likewise, we continually generate reports that help us determine whether the ministry is bearing fruit. Here is a list of the types of measurements we use in our ministry.

• **Attendance (weekly).** We review attendance trends throughout the year and compare the results with those from previous years. This information is used to analyze changes caused by factors such as message series, advertising, promotion, speakers, and service times.

• **Offerings (weekly).** Again, we review trends and compare them to previous years. We monitor per capita giving and compare those numbers to the steps people are taking in their spiritual maturity. We also monitor these numbers to measure external factors that might influence giving, including economic conditions and world and community events.

• **Attendance and revenue forecasts (weekly).** Based on the weekly attendance and offering numbers, we're also able to project future increases or decreases in either area. Good measurement tools will create snapshots of today, offer comparisons with yesterday, and help project what will happen tomorrow.

• **Spiritual steps (monthly).** We measure the number of people in our database, the weekend crowd, membership covenants, the number of people who have accepted Christ, and baptisms. This monthly report provides a snapshot of the steps people are taking in their walk with Christ.

• **Financial reports (monthly).** These include income and expense statements, balance sheets, cash-flow projections, and building-project reports. It goes without saying that ministry can't be effective unless the church is diligent about maintaining financial integrity.

• **Vision statement progress (quarterly).** This report includes items from the monthly "spiritual steps" report along with other measurements, including the number of ministry servants, small-group connections, and leadership development.

Performance measurement is one of the keys to any successful ministry. At their most basic, measurements help an organization determine what has happened. Based on that determination, and if the results are positive, leaders can decide to press on with the current ministry plan. If the results aren't positive, these measurements can stimulate decisions and actions to help improve future results.

—Tony

99 There Are No Shortcuts

"But these things I plan won't happen right away. Slowly, steadily, surely, the time approaches when the vision will be fulfilled. If it seems slow, wait patiently, for it will surely take place. It will not be delayed" (Habakkuk 2:3, NLT).

There's a danger in reading a book like this one. The same danger exists in all the conferences available to church leaders. When we learn new ideas, we may begin to think that everything can happen overnight. Yes, there are some amazing stories about how quickly God can move to cause thousands of people to gather for weekend services. The fact is, though, these instances are exceptions to the rule. Ministry is hard work no matter what size your church is.

The "normal" path includes blood, sweat, and tears. Typically, a leader will catch a vision from God and begin telling others how lives can be changed and how a community can be reached. Then the years of wrong turns, relational disappointments, and resource challenges begin.

At Granger, we've been through ten years of doing ministry in theaters and schools. We've been through at least two instances in which a handful of families who were once ministry partners decided their vision didn't match ours. We've been through dozens of situations in which staff or volunteer leaders have challenged the integrity of the mission, vision, and values; people who we thought were on our team ended up questioning whether we really knew God's will. We've been through wage freezes, budget cuts, and difficult family conversations about the financial challenges of a growing church. We've also been through personal questioning of our callings.

I'm convinced these hardships are God-ordained. Without them, our tendency would be to take control. Yet all we can do is be faithful to the calling God has given us. Pursue Jesus. Go where he tells you to go. Actively take steps to fulfill the Great Commandment and Great Commission. Pray persistently for the Holy Spirit to transform people's lives.

No, there aren't any shortcuts—just faithful service and sacrifice. Then, together, we can look forward to moving beyond these challenges to the glory God has promised will be revealed to us on the other side.

—Tony

201

Discussion Guide

One helpful way to use this book is to read it as a team. You may want to consider reading ten chapters every week for the next ten weeks. Schedule an hour to come together to discuss what you've learned and map out a plan for ministry improvements. Here are some questions to help guide your discussion.

1. In the chapters you read this week, what idea most challenged your thinking?

2. Of the principles that were covered, do you consider any to be inaccurate or inappropriate for your ministry environment?

3. Are there any obvious or easy changes that would improve the ministry effectiveness of your church? If so, what are those changes? Is there anything preventing you from implementing them immediately?

4. What insight would involve the most risk for implementation but could offer the biggest reward? Do you believe God is calling you to take that risk?

5. What is your most pressing question about the topics you've covered? Where do you need discernment or further study to know if it's a change God really wants for your church?

6. Has this week's reading caused you to consider anything in your personal leadership approach that you would like to change?

7. What action step could your ministry team take to improve the effectiveness of your church's ministry? Who will be responsible for that action step? What is your target date for implementation?

Topical Index

The Granger Story

In 1986, Mark Beeson came to Granger, Indiana, with his wife, Sheila, and their three kids. They had a vision for a ministry that would effectively reach people who either had never attended church or who thought churches were irrelevant to their lives. Mark believed a ministry could exist that is unwavering in its commitment to the truth of the gospel while using communication methods that resonate with the current culture.

For its first ten years of existence, Granger Community Church's Sunday services were held in movie theaters just down the road from the church's present location. Mark often shares the following story of how God provided that location.

When he first came to town, Mark began to invite people to join him and Sheila in small-group gatherings. Eventually the gatherings outgrew their home, so they moved to various meeting rooms in the community. Soon they had enough people to launch their first Sunday service.

Mark began to look for auditorium space in local schools. Unfortunately, at that time, the schools would not allow churches to use their facilities. It was a discouraging time because God was drawing people to this new ministry but answers weren't coming for a location in which to meet on Sunday mornings.

One day, Mark took a drive by the mall and parked his car along the main road. He recalls watching the traffic and praying for people as they drove by. Along with discouragement about the difficulty of finding a home for the church, other emotions began to kick in. Mark talks about sitting there that day, praying for people while crying about the situation. He was wondering if he had misinterpreted God's will for his ministry. Then he prayed one of those prayers of desperation: "God, just show me a sign. You know we need a place to meet for services. Just show me a sign."

After that, he recalls, he wiped the tears from his eyes and turned around to see what was going on behind him. Construction was taking place in the lot across from the mall. Equipment was moving. A building was going up. And there it was. He hadn't noticed it before. It was a sign—a big billboard that read, "Coming soon—GCC." GCC was the abbreviation and emblem for General Cinema Corporation. This company thought it was building a place for people to be entertained with movies, but God had another purpose for that building. Another GCC, Granger Community Church, began holding Sunday services there the very first day the theaters opened.

For ten years, the church gathered in the theaters for services. Every Sunday at 6:00 a.m., a group of people would unload the storage trailer and begin to convert the facility. One of the theaters was used for the service itself. The other theaters were used for children's ministry. Coffee was served from the concession counter, and people took the coffee into the services, making use of the cup holders available in the theater seats. The services included contemporary music and slide presentations on the big screen.

Mark's vision for a church to reach the unchurched began to take shape, and the ministry began to bear fruit. In 1996, the church moved from the theaters to its existing campus. The original facility has since been expanded to include a one thousand-seat auditorium and an interactive Children's Center. The church currently has over four thousand people attending services each weekend including as many as one thousand children from birth through fifth grade.

The church's influence continues to grow beyond its ministry to the people of Granger and the surrounding communities near South Bend. Part of Granger's vision is to resource other churches and ministry leaders around the world. In partnerships with Saddleback Church and the Bible League, Granger has sent staff and volunteers to India, Slovakia, and the Sudan to train and equip church leaders with its ministry strategy. Each year, the church hosts the Innovative Church Conference to help ministries learn the principles that have helped Granger reach today's culture with the unchanging truth and hope found only in Jesus Christ.

About the Authors

Tim Stevens is the executive pastor at Granger Community Church (www.gccwired.com). For nearly a decade, Tim served in various leadership positions with Life Action Ministries, including information technology, resource development, and executive management. With a growing desire to have an impact in a local church, he joined the staff at Granger in 1994. As executive pastor, he has helped the church grow from four hundred to over four thousand in weekly attendance with a staff of over forty. He has overseen four major construction projects, dozens of staff hires, and the development of the church's vision and values, branding, and strategic plan for the future. Tim was instrumental in the completion of Granger's new, interactive Children's Center, which has been featured in numerous publications for its innovative approach to reaching families.

Tony Morgan is the pastor of administrative services at Granger. After receiving a B.S. in Business Administration and a master's degree in Public Administration from Bowling Green State University in Ohio, Tony spent almost ten years serving in local government—most recently in Niles, Michigan, as city administrator. As the chief executive officer of that community, he was responsible for over 150 employees and a $20 million budget. With a growing passion to lend his gifts to help a thriving church, he transitioned into church leadership in 1998. Tony has strengthened and developed the administrative departments at Granger with creative systems, quality staff, and over 350 volunteers. He also serves on the Senior Management Team at Granger, where he contributes as a strategic thinker and practical visionary.

In addition to their roles at Granger, Tim and Tony desire to resource other ministries throughout the country. Together, they launched WiredChurches (www.wiredchurches.com), Granger's ministry to church leaders around the world. They both have presented workshops and trained other churches through conferences and consulting. Tony has also written numerous articles on staffing, technology, strategic planning, and other church leadership topics.